BORN TO SERVE

Peggy Burton

Publishers:

KHB

King's Highway Books
P.O. Box 106
Downton
Salisbury
Wiltshire
ENGLAND
SP5 3BP

Publishers :
King's Highway Books
P.O. Box 106
Downton
Salisbury
Wiltshire
ENGLAND
SP5 3BP

Copyright © 2001 Peggy Burton

This book is an 'update' on 'Challenged to Conquer', which was written and published in 1994. It now includes the history and development of the Medical Missionary Association, culminating in the creation and development of the Christian Health Professionals Resource Centre, entitled HEALTHSERVE.

Further information or more copies can be obtained from :
King's Highway Books
P.O. Box 106
Downton, Salisbury
Wiltshire, ENGLAND
SP5 3BP

Printed by :
Selsey Press Ltd
84 High Street
Selsey, Chichester
West Sussex PO20 0QH

ISBN 0-9541015-0-2

CONTENTS

Foreword
Preface
1	–	Called to serve.	8
2	–	Destination Africa.	16
3	–	Housekeeping in the jungle.	23
4	–	God's children.	28
5	–	Jungle dispensary.	37
6	–	Creating a hospital.	45
7	–	Through the valley of clouds.	54
8	–	Our disappointments and God's appointments.	65
9	–	Marley Manor and the Medical Appeal.	71
10	–	A vision realised.	78
11	–	Off the launching pad.	86
12	–	Blessings out of buffetings.	94
13	–	More cloudy valleys.	102
14	–	ECHO advances.	107
15	–	Cheaper by the million.	113
16	–	Bursting at the seams.	121
17	–	Now thank we all our God.	129
18	–	World emergencies.	135
19	–	Famine relief.	144
20	–	Growing out of all proportion.	152
21	–	Final months at ECHO.	157
22	–	To God be the glory.	164
23	–	Into retirement.	168
24	–	Eternal Love Winning Africa.	172
25	–	New opportunities.	178
26	–	Early years of the Medical Missionary Association.	183
27	–	MMA Advances through the year.	187
28	–	MMA at the crossroads.	192
29	–	HEALTHSERVE is born.	196
30	–	We are all Born to Serve.	203

Acknowledgements

Many thanks to James, my patient husband. We have spent over 50 years together serving the Lord in a variety of situations. I am so grateful for his invaluable help, expert advice and knowledge concerning ECHO and MMA. Without his help it would not have been possible to give the necessary information about these two organisations.

Foreword

By Mr Howard Lyons M.Sc.,B.Sc(Econ).,FHSM.,MIPD.
Chairman of the Medical Missionary Association.

The world in which we now live is very different from the world of 1878 when the Medical Missionary Association was founded.

In those days, it took several months to travel to parts of Africa to serve as a medical missionary. Now it takes several hours. In those days, surgery was in its infancy, anaesthetics were crude and drugs unsophisticated. Now through telemedicine, patients in Borneo and Bangladesh can be diagnosed in London and Edinburgh, surgical conditions can be treated endoscopically and powerful drugs can obviate the need for any surgical intervention.

And yet, the world's needs in this twenty-first century are so much greater. Even today, millions of children die each year from malaria, measles and diarrhoea. Thousands of women die in labour through lack of medical help. Countless numbers go blind through lack of basic healthcare. And the terrible scourge of AIDS in Africa, Asia and South America is only just beginning to register an impact in the West where the availability of expensive drugs has minimized the mortality rates.

As the world's needs are greater, so the need for healthcare missionaries is greater than ever. Trained professionals who are willing to turn their backs on lucrative careers in the UK and the West to follow in the footsteps of those who left their homes and their loved ones to serve Christ and his people in impoverished circumstances in run-down mission hospitals or community clinics. Healthcare workers who are prepared not only to share their skills and knowledge with those who cannot afford to pay even the cost of an aspirin but also through their caring, to show the love of Christ for lost sinners and to offer the words of life when given an opportunity to do so.

The Medical Missionary Association has been involved in the vital ministry of encouraging healthcare professionals to work overseas for nearly 125 years. It has had one basic objective: to mobilize Christian healthcare professionals to serve Christ and His Church in developing countries. But recognizing that the world has changed, the MMA has had to re-think how best to fulfil this vision and, in response to this, has recently launched a new Resource Centre for Christian healthcare professionals called "HealthServe".

HealthServe aims to inspire, inform and connect those who sense God's calling to medical mission with the areas of greatest need. It is a ministry first and foremost to individual spirit-filled Christians but it also serves churches and sending agencies here in the UK as well as mission posts overseas which are looking for help from trained healthcare workers.

This new edition tells the exciting story of how HealthServe came into being with the help and encouragement of James and Peggy Burton. It is a story which I trust will inspire countless numbers of Christian healthcare professionals - both young and old - to obey the great commission and go out in to all the world to make disciples of every nation using the gifts and knowledge which the Lord has given them.

Preface

From the very beginning of our Christian walk James and I have always worked together as a term, sharing joys and sorrows and continually learning new things as we have followed the pilgrim way.

Pioneering a medical work in the heart of the dense African jungle, we soon realised the desperate need for medical equipment and personnel. From this point on, our lives were geared to do something about it.

As the story unfolds, you will see how God worked out His purposes as He called us to respond to these needs amongst the poorer nations of the world.

Then came the conception and development of ECHO
(Equipment for Charity Hospitals Overseas) that was nothing short of a miracle. Retiring from this organisation after 23 years, our walk with the Lord led us through a variety of experiences until we finally became involved with the MMA (Medical Missionary Association) and the development of HEALTHSERVE. From equipment to personnel as our first vision in Africa had revealed.

Sense the excitement of the experiences we encountered as you read through the story before you. We pray that you will be stimulated, stirred and encouraged, and will be conscious of the mighty power and love of God that is readily available when each one of us follow the way He leads. Let us ALL realise that we are ALL 'BORN TO SERVE'

1 : Called to serve

'It's your turn to make the tea, Peggy,' my father called from the depths of his feather bed.

The Second World War was at its height. Mother, father and I slept in one downstairs room which was supported by huge timbers to form a kind of house shelter, which would give some protection against bomb blast. We lived in an ordinary road of semi-detached houses in the London suburb of Harrow.

'OK,' I replied sleepily. 'I'm on the way.' It was 6 a.m. on a cold November morning and I was in no hurry to extricate myself from my cosy nest of blankets and eiderdown covering. I yawned and stretched and sat up, dangling my legs over the side of the bed, making a vain attempt to find my slippers. It was cold as I stretched for my dressing gown hanging, as always, on the post of my bedhead in readiness for instant evacuation, if necessary.

Then it happened! Everything in rapid succession, so that it was difficult to know exactly what was happening. There was a shattering blast as the french doors and windows were blown out of their frames and broken glass showered across the beds, together with plaster, bricks and anything else caught up in the hurricane blast.

Without thinking what I was doing, I instinctively disappeared beneath the debris head first, back into my bed. I can vividly remember the choking sensation as I gasped for breath amidst the clouds of plaster dust which was filling the atmosphere. When the dust had settled we emerged, dazed and shattered, to shake off the debris with which we were surrounded. I remember my father - never very strong and always very nervous - having a fit of hysterics as he clambered round the room, frantically grovelling for his clothes and most distressed because he could not find his collar stud! Mother, in less of a frenzy, never did find part of her underwear!

When we eventually got out of our shattered cage, we found an even worse mess in the kitchen, and I just thanked God for my delayed action. The back door, blown off its hinges, lay across the kitchen floor just where I would have been standing by the stove making the tea. Apart from the dust and the debris, the door was neatly crowned with our breakfast kipper, which had apparently been shock blasted out of its slumber in the larder. The dresser doors had burst open to release a shower of crockery, thus adding to the chaos on the floor. Even the butter dish warming by the stove, had joined in the drama, shedding a spattering of its precious contents to decorate the shambles. As we surveyed the scene before us, it was hard to believe that we had been so near to death and destruction in a matter of so few minutes. We had, indeed, just missed a direct hit by a couple of bombs that had been released by a German bomber returning from the regular night raid on London. Presumably, he just wanted to get rid of his cargo before returning home.

While we continued wandering around discovering further damage, including a gaping hole in the roof, through which rain was now pouring, there was a bang at the front door which still remained intact.

'Are you all right?' called a voice through the letterbox. It was James; he lived only five doors down the road.

We had grown up together as children, gone to prep school together, played together, and done many things together as families in those early years, until I had been packed off to boarding school and there had been a few years of separation. Now we travelled together to London each day, to follow our separate careers. James was working as a junior at the Royal Institute of British Architects in Portland Place and I was a junior clerk in the Post Office Savings Bank, near Olympia. We never knew quite how we would get to work. Most of the time the trains kept running but if a bomb hit the line during the night, it was a question of getting there the best possible way; on one memorable occasion it was on the back of a lorry! If the bombers came over during the day, one spent much time in the underground shelters, and if there was no time to reach the shelters, then one simply ducked under a table or similar covering. Travelling home was hazardous too, and sometimes involved travelling through the night blitz; bombs and ack-ack guns lighting up the night sky, with ghostly shadows that tended to plunge one into a state of hypnotised terror and emotional stress. The rest of the evening or night would be spent under the stairs or in the shelter. Such was life in those war-torn years, that it made a lasting impression upon the individuals living and working in the heart of our big cities.

James's experience had been even more dramatic than ours. Still fast asleep in his upstairs bedroom when the bombs fell, he had been blown out of bed and hurled to the floor as the wardrobe and dressing table crashed across the room and landed upon the bed; followed by the windows and walls. Hastily flinging on what clothes he could find amongst the rubble, he scrambled to the assistance of his mother and father - the latter needing temporary treatment for head wounds caused by falling plaster - clambered over the ruins and, in his haste, tripped and fell down an open manhole in the road outside. ARP and social workers were bustling about sorting out the wounded and dishing out hot, sweet tea to the shocked and dazed residents who were wandering around in pyjamas and odd attire.

So he arrived on our doorstep, and there was a sense of great relief when we knew that both our families were intact. It was at this point that our friendship began to deepen and we realised that God had a purpose for our lives together. We had both acknowledged Jesus as our Saviour and Lord, James at a Boy Crusader Camp at the age of 12, and myself recently at a Post Office Christian Association house party. Neither of us found those early years as young Christians very easy, having all the usual problems that young Christians face. However, we joined a local Anglican Church and soon we joined in with the various church activities.

Now we wanted to serve the Lord together in reality. We became involved in the formation of a Youth Fellowship, six of us meeting in one another's homes. Later, it became a recognised part of the church. Neither of us had a lot of background knowledge, so our meetings were simple. We prayed, had Bible study, gave Gospel messages, and organised outings. We were in our element working for the Lord, and were thrilled to see our friends responding to Jesus one by one. Later, several went on to train for the ministry or mission field. Numbers grew as the weeks passed and it was all very exciting; we were blissfully happy.

One evening when I was spending time alone with the Lord, kneeling by my shelter bed, I became very conscious of a voice speaking to me. There was nothing dramatic, but I knew that this was the moment that I had to offer myself full-time, to serve and follow Him. Just as Peter and Andrew left their fishing nets to go with Jesus - indeed, many others in the Bible left what they were doing at the call of the Lord - so I realised I must respond in obedience to His call. From that moment on, without any means of explanation, I knew that my place of service was to be Africa. It was one of those moments that you can't explain to anyone else, and yet you know that something has taken place that you will never forget.

As a small child I had always had a strange fascination for Africa and even today, I can remember the little models I used to make; brown paper jungle trees with leaves sticking out of their tops, silver paper rivers running through and animals from my miniature zoo collection hiding in the undergrowth. It seems even in those early days, God was preparing me for my life's work and installing the right desires within me.

'My frame was not hidden from you when I was made in the secret place. When I was woven together in the depths of the earth, your eyes saw my unformed body. All the days ordained for me were written in your book before one of them came to be.' (Ps. 139:15, 16).

James had had a similar experience, but both our experiences were quite independent. Travelling home in a tube train one night during the blitz, he was very conscious of the Lord speaking to him.

'I want you to be a medical missionary.'

He was only an office boy in an architect's office and had just £5 in his bank account. What a ridiculous thought to go through university training with only £5! His mind was far from relaxed as he thought over this request and fought against the implications. Only a few days earlier he had quite spontaneously walked into All Souls, Langham Place, during a lunch-hour service. The title given to the message that day had been, 'Why I should not be a missionary'. This had been a challenge to him and he could not forget the words he had heard on that occasion. Now this clear call. What should he do? It all seemed so impossible. But God does not ask us to try working out the details when He wants a job done; He can cope with all those. So it was, that in that empty railway carriage, James knelt down and yielded all that he had to the Lord; himself, his meagre belongings and his £5 bank balance.

At this time, news reached him concerning his sister, Julia. She had left for Nigeria with the Church Missionary Society in 1943, travelling in a troop ship in a convoy of two ships. Both ships were bombed and most of the troops went down with the ships which sank near Casablanca, Morocco. Julia was one of the survivors who spent the following night in a lifeboat. They were picked up the next day by a Royal Navy escorting corvette and taken to an American army camp in the desert of North Africa. So Julia arrived in North Africa to serve the Lord and to proclaim the Good News of the Gospel; she had lost everything she possessed in the ordeal. The news of his sister's experience, her rescue and her faithfulness to carry out the call of her Master, made a profound impact on James. When God calls, he also equips and knows our every need.

Thus, James was soon to learn that with God, all things are possible; his £5 coped with a training which in those days amounted to £1,000 for fees alone. Holiday jobs in factories, on plantations; night fire watching in city firms; unexpected grants - the Lord provided all that was necessary and no more! Five years later, James graduated from Edinburgh University with flying colours, and we were just left standing amazed at what the Lord will do when we are obedient to the Heavenly call through the power of the Holy Spirit...

'You hem me in behind and before; you have laid your hand upon me. Such knowledge is too wonderful for me, too lofty for me to attain.' (Ps. 139:5, 6)

Nursing during the war years at Guys hospital

As for me, I had to make a firm decision about training, and without complications I was accepted by Guy's Hospital for a nursing course. Basically the training was in London, but during those war years we were constantly moved around the various wartime base hospitals. Obedience, courage and faith were essential as daily we faced death; appalling casualties were constantly being brought in, and constantly I had to seek to overcome my own fears amidst the horrors and suffering that surrounded me. This was particularly the case when I was posted to London during the period of the 'doodle bugs' and the 'V2's'. Night after night the casualties poured in, dead or alive; the underground operating theatre worked round the clock and in the morning, casualties that could be moved were transported in converted 'Green Line' buses to the base hospitals in Kent. At night in the London centre, patients who could be moved from the wards were taken into the underground shelter wards; those too ill had to remain in the wards, and we nurses took turns to stay with them. A day off meant a time to get away from the constant horrors of physical suffering, but coming back revealed once more the reality of war. I battled my way through the evening rush of Borough residents settling in to temporary bunks along the sides of the platforms in the tube stations, little children whimpering, with drawn-faced women endeavouring to comfort and calm. There was little to bring them joy or relief.

But there came a point when my physical facade of bravery gave way; I was hastily removed from duties. To get right away from London I headed for Scotland, where James had prepared a brief stay in Trossach country. He was studying at Edinburgh at the time. Oh, the bliss of the beautiful scenery and the peacefulness of nature. Why all this war and destruction? Surely God never meant it to be this way? Here, the days were relaxed and carefree as we spent time together for the first time on our own, away from family and other responsibilities; we had time to think and pray. It was becoming more and more apparent that we should consider a life of service together. We had so far experienced the abiding love and grace of God in our lives and the gentle, but firm guidance of the Holy Spirit. Now we felt His touch upon us in a very real and definite way. Without further ado, we clinched the matter and became engaged! The date was July 3 rd, 1944. We had a special time of prayer that evening; it was a marvellous time, and there was so much for which to thank our glorious Lord. We prayed with confidence and determination that from this very day, God would overrule in everything, take first place before all things in our lives, and that we would seek to be obedient, allowing the power of His Holy Spirit to control our lives in every detail. So we made our vows and, in a sense, our lives together in His Service had already begun.

I returned to my hospital duties with new enthusiasm, realising that an exciting future lay ahead, and I was determined not to let the terrors of war break me again. I did the rounds of the base hospitals; we nursed the London bomb casualties there; then the troops from the British invasion attempt who were brought to us from Dover. There was little off-duty; little time to muse upon romance! Back at base, peace was declared. I was in Outpatients at the time, I remember, and we rushed up to the flat roof top as the sirens sounded, to look out over Dockland, already colourful with waving bunting everywhere. Even today, I can still hear the wonderful sound of all the barge sirens filling the air with their cries of victory. We dashed out into the street and bought Union Jacks, already being sold by street vendors; everyone was madly excited. In the evening, a crowd of us made our way to the Palace to join the multitudes already gathering; we cheered for the King and Queen, and roared with the crowd as they appeared several times on the balcony. We had made up a band from bedpans and dishes, which we beat with a variety of instruments. Such crazy fun expressed how we felt; the release from tension, the freedom of being able to get around without being constantly alerted by the sirens. It

Wedding day, James and Peggy, August 16th 1947

all expressed so vividly what a relief it was to have peace after six long years of war. Now it was all over!

When my period at Guy's came to an end, there was just a six-month period at Queen Charlotte's Maternity Hospital to complete my training. But, at the same time, we needed to begin an important research programme of missionary societies. Through a meeting at the Tabernacle, Elephant & Castle, we were drawn towards the Regions Beyond Missionary Union, and eventually became accepted into service with them, subject to the necessary 'finishing' course to follow our medical training programme.

Our wedding took place on August 16th, 1947, and what an exceptionally hot day it was! Next day, with our bicycles, we left London by train and headed for an ecstatic honeymoon in the Lake District, followed by a necessary parting, in order to complete the final lap of our training. Whilst James went over to Belgium and studied in French to obtain a diploma in tropical medicine, I went to the Bible Training Institute in Glasgow, to improve my knowledge in theology and practical Christian studies. This was not an easy period but, as with any separation of this kind, it increased our devotion to one another and strengthened our bond of love and appreciation. It was essential that our preparation was complete before we ventured into the responsible future that lay ahead of us.

... *'I have placed before you an open door that no-one can shut; I know that you have little strength, yet you have kept my word and have not denied my name...' (Rev 3:8)*

Once we have passed through the door of opportunity that Jesus opens for us, then nothing can hinder the achievement of His purposes in our lives.

....oOo....

2 : Destination Africa

By October 1948 we were ready to leave, training complete, luggage packed, passports and documents in order and pockets empty! After the days of final preparation, valedictory meetings and farewells, the few moments together with a small group of loved ones and friends in the heart of a busy London station were very precious. Stains of the twenty-third psalm were mingled with the bustle and clutter of the smoky station atmosphere as the train slowly moved away. It was hardly surprising that emotions were aroused as, with excited expectancy, we started on the first stage of our long journey.

The sea voyage to follow was a tonic of rest, following the inevitable upheaval of leaving home. Two weeks later we were actually entering the mouth of the Congo River, the highway through the very heart of the Continent of Africa. With all its tributaries, the Congo River contributes 12,000 miles of navigable waterways and, in places, stretches to a width of 24 miles. It is dotted with more than 4,000 islands and its brown, muddy waters flow 100 miles out to sea.

As we neared the port of Matadi, we passed through the treacherous whirlpool waters, the start of many miles of intermittent cataracts that interrupt the river as it passes through the mountainous area of the lower Congo. This part of the river defies all navigation; here at Matadi we disembarked.

Only those who have experienced their first faltering steps in the land of God's choosing for their ministry can appreciate how our hearts leapt for joy the moment we set foot on dry soil - African soil. Years of training and now we were really here, standing where so many other missionaries had stood. Before the railway was built in 1898, the early pioneer missionaries and travellers had to trek inland on foot from here, over dangerous and difficult territory; there was no other way. Many of them fell ill en route and never reached their destinations; things were different now. However, the train journey was quite an ordeal; it took all day to reach Leopoldville. The seats were hard and it was very hot, but to keep the windows open meant a constant breeze of black smuts. This one-track railway took us through magnificent mountain scenery, opening out into grassland with beautiful views; we stopped at little 'halts', which were alive with the hustle and bustle of African life.

Leopoldville was the capital city of the Belgian Congo, with towering buildings, broad boulevards and modern stores. That was the European sector; the African sector was squalid in comparison. It was necessary to spend six weeks in Leopoldville to complete a brief hospital training, at the end of which James would receive a certificate of recognition, allowing him to practise in the Belgian Congo as an Accredited Doctor. We also explored some of the surrounding villages and countryside, and made some food and home purchases to be shipped up river.

So the day eventually arrived for us to board the 'Reine Astride', an old Mississippi stern-wheel paddle steamer with four decks. This journey took us four days. Our 40 pieces of luggage had been carefully checked and, somehow, we managed to pack 23 of them into our tiny cabin, under bunks and in every available space. There was a little basin in the cabin too, but the water was from the river so it was necessary to have some filtered drinking water with us; it stayed permanently warm in the stuffy, humid atmosphere, but at least it helped to quench our thirst.

The 'Reine Astride' was a wood-burning vessel and stopped every night to take on the next day's fuel supply. This operation took most of the night, wood being hurled into the hold, and the Africans chanting and shouting as they worked. It so happened that our cabin was centrally situated over the wood storage space, and so we got the full force of the exercise. As the pile got higher, each successive log hit the cabin floor and we began to expect, any moment, to see one shoot through the floorboards! This continued until 3 or 4 a.m., then the deck swabbing crew took over, and the fire was built up under the boiler to get up steam for the next part of the journey. Then there was more chanting as the boat pulled out of its moorings to the rhythmic beating of the paddle-wheel and the soft, puffing sound of the engine. Now we could get some sleep as the steamer chuffed steadily on into the dawn. Throughout the day, hour after hour, the panorama of wide, brown murky river, innumerable small islands and masses of blue water hyacinth, was unending. One day, we noticed a canoe, flying a blue flag with a golden star - the national navigation flag - coming towards us. The engines of the stern-wheeler slowed down as the little canoe drew alongside, and a large mail sack was tossed on board. A similar sack was tossed from the steamer into the canoe, narrowly missing the water. Greetings were exchanged before the 'postman' turned his canoe and headed for shore. So much for the Congo postal service! Even today medical supplies are continually being sent in this way to isolated stations; I wonder how many are treated in like manner?

The river was very wide in this part and there were many islands. The hills got smaller as gradually we were making our way into the Central Congo Basin, which is covered by the great equatorial forest and huge natural palm groves. Here and there we glimpsed a village, and an occasional canoe or other craft; a mysterious quiet hung over the river.

A blast from the stern-wheeler warned us that we were drawing into shore for a brief stop at a small settlement and important river junction. Already a crowd had gathered on the grassy slopes. Four men dived off the bow of the boat into the muddy water, hauling with them a great steel landing cable, which they fastened to a tree. This performance was repeated at the stern. A gangway was lowered and two planks pushed along to bridge the remaining gap. Immediately, there was an evacuation of excited, chattering Africans, clamouring down the gangway with buckets, babies and baskets. There was then a mad rush to buy up dried fish, fruit, manioc, etc. Little time was allowed for the exchange of goods and, after a very short stay, the siren sounded and a frantic, hustling crowd tried to sort itself out with almost disastrous results. A man precariously balanced on the gangway with a large bunch of unsold bananas; a mother pushed her way into the middle of the plank with an unconcerned baby firmly secured on her back and almost unfooted a young lad who had been trying to sell eggs on board. So the clatter went on, until all were safely sorted out and once again the gangway went up, cables were loosed and the stern-wheeler nosed her way towards midstream. Such was the experience at stop after stop along the way.

We made a brief stop at the State Company Post and Mission station of the Baptist Missionary Society at Bolobo, and just had time to meet the missionaries and have a quick glimpse round the hospital where, to our amazement, patients were stretched out on and under the beds! This was our first glimpse of a bush hospital and we were immediately shattered by the simplicity, the primitive conditions and the apparent lack of facilities and equipment. It was all so different to what we were used to at home!

We continued on our way to Coquilhatville, where we were to leave the big Mississippi boat to board a smaller one, only a fraction of the size, to negotiate one of the smaller tributaries of the Congo River, along which our first destination was located. The quayside at Coquilhatville was a busy hive of activity as luggage, cargo and post were loaded and unloaded to and from the boat, conveyed into smaller boats or carried into large warehouses.

Everyone seemed to be shouting or arguing over something; everyone thinking that everyone else ought to be carrying a load! Lorries and cars clattered over the rough quayside, and passengers dodged in and out between activities.

The boat we now boarded had only two cabins for Europeans, and one for the captain; conditions were very primitive. The underside of the boat was flat, almost level with the water; the engine and wood stores were under the cabins and the paddle wheel at the stern, and there was a very small deck for sitting and eating. Four metal-topped barges were attached to the boat; one on either side and two in front. These contained freight boxes and oil drums and served as deck space for the African passengers and crew, who occupied the lower deck. Their accommodation was very cramped by the time they had packed their baskets, cooking pots, tin trunks, bed mats, chickens, ducks and goats, into every available space.

So, we set off on the last lap of our river journey. As we travelled on, we left the great stretches of the broad Congo River and penetrated right into the heart of the African jungle. There was little to do now, except to read and relax, or just to gaze at the continuity of dense tropical forest on either side of the narrowing river; thick creepers and undergrowth lined the banks below tall forest trees. It was easier now to catch a glimpse of animal, reptile and bird life. Parrots in the tree tops and brightly coloured sunbirds and kingfishers darted across the water. Monkeys chattered as they crashed from branch to branch; water buck darted back into the thick undergrowth. Sometimes a hippo surfaced or crocodiles were seen sunning themselves on the occasional sandy patch alongside the banks. We were thankful that our craft was substantial enough to withstand any possible attack. But, on the whole, the river was quiet and somewhat melancholy here, as we chugged on through the smooth, dark waters.

Every sundown the boat anchored alongside a tiny refuelling station which was nothing more than a clearing where thousands of short logs had been collected and arranged in regular stacks to be loaded on to these wood-burning boats. Travelling in the dark was unwise, as the boat could easily hit a sand bank. As the sun set, it did so with a fierce intensity, sharpening the outline of the forest, turning the rippling water into pools of dark mystery; a fine setting for all the sounds of nocturnal wildlife which made up the African night chorus. Tiny fireflies flickered about like minute specks of light and mosquitoes buzzed incessantly. Long before dawn we were on our way once more. The air was cool at this time of the morning, and a thin mist hung over the water as, imperceptibly, the darkness faded and the trees became visible once more. Suddenly, the forest came to life; the birds were singing and alert and the monkeys started their incessant chatter; another day had begun.

Each day we passed the occasional village; with a 'whoop-whoop' the boat siren would penetrate the still air and the people would scurry down to the riverbank to wave to us until we passed out of sight. Sometimes a canoe or two would be paddled out to the sides of the barges and traders would sell crocodile or monkey meat , fish or vegetables, to the passengers. We stopped sometimes at one or other of the villages, for time seemed no object and schedules were immaterial. So the days passed, until we finally arrived at our first destination. The trip had taken just one week from Coquilhatville. There was the usual clatter of excitement with crowds of people chattering as they came and went, chickens clucking and goats bleating, just to add to the commotion. We were met by the missionaries, hospital staff, singing school boys and a large 'welcome' banner. We were overwhelmed by such love and kindness and tried to reciprocate by making our first faltering attempts to greet them in their own tribal tongue.

We now had to spend a period of time in language study and hospital technique, learning how to manage with much less equipment and fewer supplies than we had been used to in the UK, often adapting things to fit a particular medical situation or emergency.

Six months later, we were on the move again; this time to our final destination. Most of our belongings were packed into a one-ton truck, together with one or two passengers balanced precariously amongst the boxes. Here, in the heart of the African jungle we passed through some of the most primitive parts of the Congo. The road was rough and often overgrown, with occasional anthills hidden in the grass; these caused considerable damage to a truck axle if unnoticed. From time to time we passed pedestrians quietly moving in the heat of the day, women carrying heavy loads on their heads, often with a baby on their back as well. They hastened back into the undergrowth as we passed. We crossed over 157 precarious log bridges as we approached the final stretch of road nearing our destination. The magnificent dense forest scenery on either side of the road was broken here and there by little villages of thatched mud huts.

We had come to this area as a direct result of a disaster which had occurred some months previously. Joseph Bolanga was Pastor at Yuli; Trixie Broom was a trained nurse who built up the medical work there. Both were killed in a plane crash at Libenge, Belgian Congo, 60 miles from Leopoldville, en route for Europe in 1948. They were on their way to a Missionary Conference in Brussels and were then going to travel to England.

The people at Yuli had asked Joseph Bolanga to plead with the people in

England to send a doctor to help them. He was never able to make that request, but James and I were sent to Yuli in answer to the prayers of the people. Thus, we took up the reins where they had left off, and sought to the best of our ability through the power of the Holy Spirit, to fulfil the longings and desires of them both.

Pioneer medical work in an isolated area over 250 km from the nearest hospital appealed to our adventurous spirits, and we were determined to make a go of it! The prayers and requests of these people were now actually being answered and there was great excitement as we arrived. It was a very moving experience to see even those who were too old to move from their huts waving and cheering as we passed.

A village near to our first home

A few miles from the mission station the road narrowed into what seemed almost like a woodland path, and we literally had to manoeuvre the truck in and out amongst the trees and potholes. The villages were almost empty now, but there were floral decorations everywhere. As we neared the mission there must have been hundreds in the crowds lining the entrance road, singing and cheering as we drove between them. Royalty could not have had a more enthusiastic welcome. 'Their' doctor had arrived at last!

We were greeted by Miss Nellie Hadaway and Miss Elsie Saunders, who had been the only two missionaries on this little station for some years.

Then the long walk down the avenue, lined with smiling, happy, black faces; we shook hands and exchanged greetings with as many as we could. At the end of the avenue there were the school children; a group of some hundred strong, singing an African song of greeting under a banner of welcome, written in Bantu script. It was a fantastic sight and so moving, as two of the children came forward to offer us gifts of flowers. The mission staff, grouped on an enormous anthill, sang a welcome too. From every direction people came streaming across the compound to greet us with welcoming handshakes; the excitement was overwhelming. The next day, Chiefs from the Yuli district arrived with gifts from the people: 33 chickens, 54 eggs, and a duck! There were speeches and greetings and thanks all round. Then there was a welcome service in the little chapel on Sunday morning. The open-sided brick building was packed to overflowing; people were everywhere, on the windowsills and outside too. We managed a brief welcome between us in simple Lomongo - the language of the people in that particular area of the country.

This then, was the opening chapter of a long story. A story through which God was going to work His purposes out; the purposes He had planned for our lives. Little did we think as we created that first bush hospital, that the Lord was going to use us in later years to help hundreds of medical causes like this one, or that those tiny Congo paddle steamers would one day be used to transport major items of medical equipment from the UK. Nor did we realise then that we had, in fact, embarked upon a long training programme to prepare us for a ministry which would grow to have a worldwide outreach, started because a few people had pleaded with their Pastor to ask for a doctor. For, as that Pastor laid down his life with his missionary colleague, the seed was sown in the hearts of many people to send a doctor to answer the cries of God's children in the heart of Africa. All because of this, needy people in underdeveloped countries all over the world are now receiving help which otherwise they might never have had. It is humbling to think that God had already planned the programme He wanted us to carry out and that He had chosen the instruments He wanted to prepare.

....oOo....

3 : Housekeeping in the jungle

There were three missionary homes at Yuli; the houses were very simple - three large rooms and three small rooms, a balcony and flight of steps back and front, thatched roof and no ceilings. The houses were set up on stone pillars, upon which were wide sheets of metal to prevent the approach of termites. These 'white ants' would rapidly destroy the wood and thatch structure if not kept in check. A cookhouse was built separate from the main building, on an extension of the back balcony, and the 'wee house' was also built in mud and sticks some thirty yards from the house; this was a home for a whole variety of creepy crawlies! Our furniture was simple, made from local wood or wicker, and we added a few comforts such as cushions, floor rugs, curtains, ornaments and a few pictures. The 'bathroom' consisted of a tin tub, a bowl on a shelf, with jug and bucket to transport water and waste.

So, this was to be our very first home and we realised that it would be very different to setting up home in the UK. For the first six months there were just the four of us: Nellie Hadaway, in charge of station affairs, Elsie Saunders, in charge of the school, James and I in charge of the dispensary and with the daunting task of creating a 'hospital'. We did not see another European during those first six months but, as time went on, news got round the district that a doctor had arrived and we began to have a few visitors: Belgians from nearby plantations, Portuguese from village stores, Catholic Fathers on isolated outposts and Belgian State personnel. Sometimes we were sent for to see a sick European, which occasionally necessitated hospitalisation in the European hospital 200 km away.

Let me tell you about some of the amusing encounters we had with African wild life. When we returned home at night after an evening out, we would always be confronted with dozens of large, shiny mahogany-brown cockroaches with long, twitching antennae, scurrying to take cover. They spent their day-time hours congregating in cupboards or dark corners, eating paint off picture frames and furniture, or chewing book covers. In the cookhouse after dark, there was an energetic obstacle race as these creatures rushed in and out of saucepans and cooking utensils. The thatched roof too housed a variety of wild life. One night a couple of lizards were having a fight on a cross-beam; they lost their balance and landed in the middle of the dining room table whilst we were having supper. The skirmish continued until one lizard got hold of the tail of the other who then simply parted company with his tail and rushed off across the table, the attacker in hot pursuit; the unfortunate tail, left behind, continued a little wiggly dance all on its own! It is a system that lizards have for getting away from an enemy.

Another night, one of the gauze doors was left open, and a swarm of ants on nuptial flight was attracted by the hurricane light and came rushing in, to land in our soup! The tiny red food ants got into everything, especially the sugar. Our gauze-sided 'larder' had to stand in tins of paraffin. There were weevils in the flour; nothing could ever be left unguarded and there were no refrigerators in those days. All water had to be boiled and filtered and we were constantly on the look-out for fleas, bugs and lice, so prevalent in the village homes.

Our beds were fitted with mosquito nets. They not only served their purpose but also kept out other insects and pests. It was not at all unusual to have rats around at night; often measuring 24 inches from tip of nose to tip of tail. They pinched the soap too! On one occasion we were woken by peculiar rustling sounds. James crawled out of the mosquito net to investigate and was met by a shower of 'bafumbi' (driver ants) and half-chewed insects dropping from the roof. We had been invaded by driver ants and they were everywhere; we had to evacuate the house.

Driver ants move from place to place, but form temporary resting homes for days at a time, usually at the base of a tree stump or root. From this central spot columns of ants radiate, moving in orderly precision to search for any living things in that particular area; then a signal is given for the ants to spread. Some attack animals or insects, and cut off sizeable pieces; the other ants carry the pieces back along the columns. To watch the ants coming and going is equivalent to watching a busy thoroughfare in the rush hour, or a miniature army on the march; those coming to the site of attack on one side; those returning to the nest on the other side, all very orderly and regimented. There are always a number of bigger 'guard' or 'soldier' ants that travel along with the rest of the column; they are twice the size of the 'worker' ants, with extra large heads that have vicious, needle-sharp pincers. These ants stand guard over the column and encourage the workers to spread out when food is detected. This operation usually takes place at night and, when the hunt is over, some kind of a signal is given and the ants leave their place of attack to march in orderly fashion back to base.

Mosquitoes were a constant threat and one had to take regular tablets to avoid an attack of malaria, and elephant flies had the habit of nipping one's legs under the dining table. There were tsetse flies and mason wasps, hornets and a host of other varieties; they all had a bite or a sting of some kind. Stick and leaf insects were numerous and lived up to their names, being quite indistinguishable from their habitat. There were several varieties of praying mantis, easily recognised by the peculiar form of the front legs, lifted as if in prayer, but also adapted for seizing and holding their prey. They eat other insects and even small lizards; they hunt by hypnosis and become fierce if annoyed, bristling up the wings and attacking with sharp jaws.

To have a bath, we used a tin tub and water was warmed for the occasion in a bucket on the cookhouse stove. Tarantula spiders seemed to like hiding in the bath tub, so careful investigation was necessary before taking a bath. They had the habit of jumping as well as walking, which made their movements unpredictable.

One night, a snake wound its way round the bed post; that caused a disturbance! Another night, James jumped out of bed and stepped right into the middle of a large, slippery snake! There were pythons, cobras, vipers and various other deadly snakes around, but normally these did not trouble us too much. One evening, a fruit bat flew into the house; they can be quite dangerous because of their sharp bite, and they are very large. We got a lad to come and shoot it with his bow and arrow; he then carried it off with great delight to cook and eat! Lizards were plentiful and there were chameleons too, that move much more slowly and change colour according to the background. Leopards prowled about at night, the most feared and hated of animals; they would raid a village and carry off chickens, goats, dogs and sometimes a child.

There was quite a farmyard on the station. Goats wandered around freely in the daytime, whilst chickens and ducks were usually kept in an enclosure for safety against attacks from civet cats and other wild animals. The bird life was very fascinating; parrots, weaver birds, pretty little red birds, tiny colourful sunbirds, black and white wagtails, herons, kingfishers, eagles and many more. We kept a monkey for a while, but she became too mischievous and would rush through the house deliberately knocking all the flower vases over or scattering ornaments; she pinched bananas hanging up on the back balcony and took a delight in hurling oranges at our little dog, or jumping on her suddenly and pulling her ears for fun!

Housekeeping was very different. We did not have a lot of meat for the simple reason that there was nothing very suitable apart from snake cutlets, stewed monkey, elephant steaks, jugged porcupine, fried alligator, roast antelope, wild boar, leopard or goat and guinea fowl, fat caterpillars, locusts, rats, lizards, ants, worms and bats, all to be found on the African menu! So we mainly stuck to chicken, goat, antelope and porcupine or fish. Eggs were also plentiful and could be bought by bartering such things as tins or old magazines.

There was an abundance of fresh fruit and homegrown vegetables, and a delicious African dish could be made with green, spinach-type leaves, mixed with palm oil; 'banganju', they called it. When a palm tree was cut down, we enjoyed palm cabbage made from the very heart of the young frond shoots, and delicious with a white sauce. There were peanuts, palm nuts, coconuts, oranges, lemons, grapefruits, citrons and tangerines; guavas, mangoes, melons, paw-paw, coeur de boeuf, pineapples, bananas, plantains, breadfruit and sugar cane. Basic vegetables were spinach, cabbage, peas, beans, sweet potato, tomatoes and cucumbers. Bread was made most days, cakes and biscuits when needed. Tinned goods and groceries in general had to be ordered from the city and stored.

The constant, humid atmosphere created mould and rust which affected books, shoes and cameras in particular, and ruined a lot of other things. If termites did get into the house, they could do a lot of damage in a short while. On one occasion when we went for a brief holiday, they ate all our dirty washing left in a wooden container, because the washboy decided not to do the washing straight away. Such was life; we just learnt to accept it! Normally, our washboy was excellent at his job, using an enormous charcoal iron. There were various other 'boys' to help with household duties. They all had to be taught how we wished to live, and it was very difficult sometimes to convey our instructions to a young lad, raw from village life. They failed to understand why we needed to live any differently from them.

One day, James was supervising the cleaning of the 'wee house' because, apart from other livestock normally taken for granted, there were a lot of hornets in the thatched roof, so we decided that they had better be removed. He set off a DDT bomb and, a few hours later, armed with brushes and sticks, James and the houseboy prepared for invasion. It was not long before an anxious-faced James returned to base, flushed and looking decidedly ruffled.

'Have we another broomhead?' he asked. 'The other one has fallen down the hole!'

I was highly amused.

'Don't you realise,' he continued, 'we have been living in imminent peril of our lives, and all you can do is laugh. There was an enormous hornet's nest just under the seat, about an inch from the rim. I was only trying to help!'

So much for the spring cleaning!

One of the fortnightly highlights of home life in the Congo was the arrival of the mail, which brought with it the thrill of a link with loved ones and friends and news of the outside world. Letters, magazines, packages - such excitement! Our postboy had to cycle 150 km, then travel by canoe for nearly a day, then walk a further 15 km to the State Post, where he picked up the mail sack. We used to send a tin trunk for the river journey, to prevent the sack from getting soaked. Even so, the trunk fell into the river from time to time and we then had to spend some time drying out the mail before we could read it.

Slowly, we began to fit into the way of life in the heart of the African forest. It was a very new experience and there were times when we longed for the home comforts and security we had left behind, the many friends and the promise of a flourishing job and secure future. But we were here at the command of our Lord and Master Jesus Christ, who had no other plan to spread the Good News of the Love of God and of Salvation, other than relying on His followers. We were two of His followers and were simply starting out on our life's work for Him.

It is true that missionary work can easily be glamorised, but serving suffering humanity is not a romantic pursuit, especially in such primitive conditions. This chapter is meant not only to give a glimpse into the conditions and circumstances of earlier missionary days, but also to show what many missionaries all over the world are facing today. In the developing days of ECHO's work, one of our main aims was to relieve the discomforts of the missionary army and give them the satisfaction of knowing we cared for their needs. Basically, we served the medical arm of missionary work, but new areas of relief and help were constantly being devised to assist the overall missionary programme.

....oOo....

4 : God's children

The lives of the people in this area, on the whole, were enveloped in fear, distrust and superstition. They often appeared to be carefree, but deep within their consciences was a sense of impending doom. They pursued their ancient ways of life, their lives encased within a mystical shroud of cults and customs. Even before established Christian missions, the early tribes of central Africa believed in God as Supreme Being of creation and power. God was then thought of as a personal deity, who rewarded the good and punished the wicked.

There were lesser gods or spirits in the mountains, forests and rivers; and other spiritual forces attributed to nature, important human beings and ancestors. Then there were forces with which magic and medicine were concerned. Man was therefore surrounded by all these powers that affected his life, family and work. Faith in fetishes made from birds' claws, feathers, a crocodile foot, teeth, horn or human hair, was very strong in some areas of Africa. There is still belief today that they are able to cure and protect from disease, guard against emotional upsets and fear, provide extra strength, ensure a good journey or even secure the safety and prosperity of a village. It was the area of primitive spiritual forces that particularly clashed with the modern medical care we were endeavouring to carry out, and with which the Medicine man had an advantage over the European doctor.

Faith in the Medicine man was tied up to a large extent with their religious beliefs and he held tremendous sway over the people. He had a great knowledge of medicines derived from herbs, roots, barks, juices and leaves, and would spend long hours dispensing pastes, ointments, brews and potions.

These people acted as if they were never quite prepared for death; no one could pass away in peace. The wailing relations, often plastered in mud and dust, would show grief even before a person died. I vividly remember one occasion in our district. A village elder died and there was a great uproar. The body was buried in a secluded spot and was covered by a small, thatched shelter in which all his belongings and a daily supply of food were

The African Medicine man

displayed for use by the departed soul in the next world.

Some weeks later, groups from many villages came together to pay their respects at an ancient 'death ceremony', created to please the spirits of the deceased. The village was gaily decorated with forest flowers and palm fronds. To the familiar drum beat of Africa, a warrior leader, clad in animal skins and charms, leapt backwards into a prepared clearing followed by a group of vividly painted and decorated dancers, moving towards him with stiff, jerky steps. Some carried spears, shields or rattles; some women had bewildered, yelling babies fastened on to their backs. As the noise and pace increased, dust rose in clouds as many feet pounded the sandy earth and the onlookers were caught up in the emotion of the moment. There was evil in the flashing eyes and harsh expressions; this was Africa behind the scenes, a world of its own. Then, as suddenly as it had started, everything calmed down; the drums ceased and the people disappeared behind the huts. But very soon the whole performance started again with another group of dancers representing another village, with their leader, a specially chosen man of high regard. Finally, all the groups united in one grand finale; a spectacular display of frenzy and excitement.

There must have been two hundred villages in an area the size of Wales for which Yuli was medically responsible. It does not take much thought to realise the impossible task of visiting these on a regular basis. Most of the villages were off the road, and to reach them involved a long trek through the forest on foot or bicycle. Others were situated on the river or a nearby lake. To get to these meant a long journey by boat or canoe, and it was not possible to be away from the mission for any length of time.

We tried to establish small dispensaries throughout the district as soon as we had adequately trained suitable male nurses to post in the villages. They had to be able to make simple diagnoses, give basic treatments, stitch up simple cuts, incise abscesses and give medicines. More difficult cases had to be sent into the mission. The other problem was that we hardly had enough equipment and drugs to keep our own dispensary work going, so it was difficult to equip these outlying dispensaries too.

We started by setting up a dispensary in a village which we could visit most weeks, but road conditions were so bad, especially in the wet season, that we could never be sure how long we would be away. There were ruts and potholes and mud, and many times we had to put leaves and branches under the wheels to get ourselves mobile again. There were many little bridges over small streams. These were made of round poles which were constantly being attacked by termites or borers, weakening the poles and causing them to give way under a heavy vehicle. It was always advisable to stop and test the bridge by jumping on it before driving over it!

When we did get a reasonably flat surface so that we could make some headway, it was not unusual for a pack of baboons to appear suddenly and dash across the road in front of us, but on approaching a village anything could happen. Goats had a habit of appearing from nowhere and once one leapt out in front of our van, causing us to swerve. The road was wet and slippery after a storm, the wheels spun round, slithered across the road broadside, narrowly missing a palm tree, and came to rest in a three-foot ditch. Two hours later, thirty strong men lifted the vehicle back on to the road again. But by now the mud had churned up on the road and it was difficult to get going again.

Trees across the road were quite a common occurrence and this could cause much delay. Once we drove over what seemed to be a thin tree, but it turned out to be a thick python! Often we had punctures and discovered that to stuff the tyre with leaves made a temporary repair, until we could get a proper repair job done. On one occasion the roof rack slid off in front of us, going down a hill. We managed to make new metal caps for the fixtures with fizzy water bottle tops. Anyone travelling or living in Africa has to have a very adaptable mind!

There was one place where we had to cross the river. This was done by ferry, which consisted of a row of planks nailed across four canoes. A very insecure looking ramp had to be set in position, then, with careful negotiating, the vehicle would be driven on to the ferry boat. -There was nothing to prevent it going straight over the rocking platform of planks into the river beyond!- The vehicle was then securely fixed for the trip across the river, carried out by several paddlers, who chanted river songs and made a great hullabaloo all the way across.

There was always a huge crowd waiting for us in the village dispensaries. Many of the people had genuine complaints which we were able to treat, but many more came with complaints that seemed quite non-existent; some of these were not sick at all. Why did they come? The answer appeared to be that they did not want the doctor to think that he had come all that way for nothing! But, despite these malingerers, there was always a great medical need in the villages. Advanced cases of leprosy, ulcers, hydroceles to be tapped, injections to be given for various things, worms and Yaws, midwifery cases, sick babies, etc. We tried to persuade prospective mothers to go to the mission for their deliveries, but it was very difficult to make them realise how inadequate and unhygienic their methods really were. The local midwives knew nothing beyond the concoction of herbs and the invocation of the spirits, and were quite helpless if there was a complication. Diagnosing and prescribing treatment was not easy in these forest villages; the language differed from village to village according to the tribe and each consultation became a long, confusing babble with everyone joining in, and one hoped to be understood adequately by the end of a complicated system of signs and interpretations.

It was our custom to hold a brief evangelistic service during our visit to the dispensary. We would call the people together by the drum language and they would gather with us under the shade of the trees. They did not hurry, but sauntered across the compound with all the time in the world. We soon learnt that you could never hurry the African; in a sense, with the constant heat and humidity, they were much more sensible than we were. The kiddies ran hither and thither or clung to their mother; goats, dogs, chickens and ducks added colour, noise and distraction, as did the crying babies, but we learnt to get used to such things; they were all part of life. Some of the women wore bright wraps, while others wore little more than a loin band. The men gathered together in a separate group, some carrying their hunting spears while the old men sat around smoking tobacco, quite often grown in front of their huts. What a wonderful privilege and opportunity to bring more than just medicine to these people, whose cares and thoughts centred around the daily routine; to bring them news of a love which could heal the greatness sickness of all. It was at times like this when all the hard work, the strange and often difficult circumstances, were worthwhile.

There were the faithful few who were believers, and they sought against all the forces of evil to proclaim the glorious news of the Gospel; those who had branched out into the lonely places to teach and evangelise, to live and work amongst their own people and to proclaim the unsearchable riches of Christ.

There was something about these forest villages that held our imagination and interest. Basically, there was an air of tranquillity and peace because time just did not seem to exist as we know it, but on the surface, a forest village in action was anything but peaceful; even at night the drums often accompanied dancing into the early hours. At the start of the day, however, the village appeared deserted. The women would tie their babies on to their backs and, together with their toddlers and daughters, go off to their gardens a short distance from the village to weed and hoe, to plant peanuts, maize, sugar cane, bananas, etc. Then they would gather firewood and fill their gourds with water. The men and the older boys would go off into the forest with their hunting nets, bows and arrows, taking their hunting dogs with them, while others went to attend to their fishing traps in the swamp or river. The only folks remaining in the village at this time would be the old or the sick, together with the goats, chickens and ducks.

However, as the people returned from their work, life returned with a vengeance. The men, with a great deal of noise, would divide their meat or fish, while the women prepared the daily meal, pounding the manioc roots and lighting fires under big clay cooking pots in which they would cook the manioc and leaves mixed with palm oil, adding meat or fish or hot peppers. Children would run about everywhere to add to the hubbub and the animal population would play its part in the drama. A wandering goat would pinch someone's manioc leaves and run off across the compound with an angry housewife in hot pursuit, heaving chunks of firewood at the thief. At the same time, the flying missile might send a cluster of chickens flying in all directions, to disturb the domestic bliss of some other family scene.

Some of the old men would return with bundles of palm fronds, a special kind for making roof mats; others with large bunches of palm nuts. These nuts were sold to the Companies for making soap and margarine; trucks came round to the village to collect the nuts every week. Many of the women spent time making clay pots from a certain kind of clay collected from the swamps. There was house building to be done as well; repairs were seldom carried out. If a house was falling down it was just left to rot and a new one would be built of sticks, mud and thatch.

As the evening wore on, the men would gather together in the village meeting house. Here they would drink a special forest brew made from berries, or palm wine, whilst they exchanged stories and told about their hunting and fishing adventures of the day. They would also prepare their hunting and fishing nets for the next day as they talked together. The

Tribal dancers

women would chatter in loud, unmelodious voices until eventually, as night descended, they would retreat to their houses to sleep.

When the moon was shining brightly, everyone was happy. Out would come the drummers, squatting with their instruments between their legs, clapping out a rhythm with their hands. Then would come the dancers, performing intricate steps while their bodies swayed rhythmically to the drum beats. Everyone would sing and chant; there seemed no time for sleep and rest.

Sometimes we had to follow a narrow track into a village through dense forest, when the boughs of the tall trees interlaced overhead and were hung with great festoons of climbing vines. The sky was barely visible and light came from thin, pencil rays of sunlight penetrating through the occasional gap in the foliage of the trees. Undergrowth rose to a height of fifteen feet high, while many trees stood 100 to 150 feet high, and there were ferns that grew several feet high too. The air in the forest was cool and damp; the path underfoot, a carpet of rotting humus. The musty smell of dead, fallen trees mixed with the scent of fresh growth and sap from newly broken branches. Orchids hung from the trees and butterflies added colour. Here one could shake off the sense of time and hurry and just be absorbed in the mystery and beauty; the forest was alive with exciting sights and sounds.

Thousands of tiny eyes were everywhere; little red spiders, crickets, beetles with exotic blue and purple shiny wings, giant wood ants and miniature ground ants. A variety of flies and mosquitoes buzzing everywhere; the forest was alive and in constant motion. There were lizards and snakes of varying shades; there was the tapping of the woodpecker and the screeching of the hornbill. The persistent call of the honeybird and thousands of little birds in vivid colours which could only be appreciated when a shaft of light glistened upon them.

Sometimes we saw monkeys flashing through the tree-tops, chattering in ceaseless conversation, brown, black and white; sometimes an antelope flashed across the path, no bigger than a small dog.

There were the sunny glades, ablaze with wild flowers and butterflies. Near to the village were the man-made clearings, where the women cultivated their gardens and grew produce for their daily needs: manioc, plantain, bananas, palm nuts, paw-paw, ground nuts, sweet potato, oranges and many kinds of tropical fruits. It was a constant battle to prevent the gardens from becoming overgrown.

The people knew how to distinguish vines which had nutritious, sweet roots, and berries that were edible. They knew the sounds that told them where the bees had hidden their honey, the exact movements of the termites and the time to catch them to provide a favourite delicacy. We wandered along the paths that led through the mysterious, leafy highway of the African forest; a world of its own, full of beauty and wonder.

On one of our itineraries we got involved with an elephant herd. We were near a river and were suddenly confronted with two large bull elephants who scented us out, threw their trunks high and screamed. They spread their wide ears and swished their tails, rocked backwards and forwards and were obviously prepared to charge. We swung our vehicle round to make a rapid retreat, only to be confronted by the rest of the herd coming up from the river, complete with mothers, aunties and babies. We swung around again, searching for an outlet, the bulls roaring furiously. There was only one hope and we took it. Heading straight for the herd, we shot through the middle of them where there was a small gap. As we looked back we observed the bulls, crashing through the undergrowth. They gave short, enraged roars, skidded to a halt near a large bush and battered it to pieces. They obviously thought we were the bush; fortunately, elephants do not have good sight!

Some of the villages in our district had to be visited by river, and one trip was quite an experience. Yuli was four miles from the start of the creek and this was approached by a rough track. Our luggage was packed together in big bundles and fastened on to long poles, each pole being carried by two men. We stayed the night in a little hut near the creek, so that we could make an early start the next day. At 3.30 a.m. the following morning, the drums beat up the paddlers and we had to get our belongings packed into the canoe. It was a tight squeeze but, as dawn began to appear, we started through the fairyland forest swamp. The creek was really a spread of water split into many small streams through the forest.

We and our baggage were packed under a thatched shelter over the centre of the canoe. Ten paddlers at the back pushed off and the 'guide' man at the front worked in unison with them. The morning light was just breaking through the trees as the paddlers guided our canoe in and out of the tree stumps, under the low hanging branches and on to the main river. We had to sit very still, for unnecessary movement in a canoe can cause havoc! The men knew all the bends of the river and would turn off the main river from time to time, and take a short cut through another creek. The sun glistening on the water cast rays of light as it broke through the thick foliage overhead and occasionally lit up the brilliant green, mossy trunk of a big tree. There were no villages for miles because at this point most of the forest was under water. Sometimes in these creeks we would get stuck on a hidden tree trunk or sandbank. Such a chatter evolved between the paddlers, as we precariously rocked around until they got us safely back into the water and afloat again. One of our main annoyances was the constant attack by tsetse flies; these insects have a painful sting.

As we went on our way, we heard distant thunder and the wind roaring through the trees. Then came the rain; it just sheeted down, but the paddlers carried on, chanting as they went, and we competed with them by singing choruses. The thunder crashed and the lightening flashed, the water was choppy and the wind lashed waves into the canoe so that our feet were soon awash. We were constantly on the watch too, for crocodiles or hippos, for they were so strong it would be quite possible for them to upturn the canoe, but the noise of the paddlers helped to keep them at bay.

We eventually came to our destination and pulled on to the beach of the village. Here we tended the sick, giving injections, dressing wounds and doing all the usual dispensary chores, giving advice and seeking to bring comfort to these forest people. There was so much suffering in the villages and so few to help. Then we went back into the canoe for the homeward trip, experiencing all the joy of serving Jesus amongst the forest tribes.

So we had opportunities to reach the people far and wide; often there was an emergency when we were called away to attend to a person in a nearby village, too sick to move. We would do what we could; how we longed for an ambulance on these occasions, or a mobile dispensary and trained staff to help us in the work. In some cases, because of the distance and the inability of the patient to reach us, or us to reach the patient, he just died.

....oOo....

5 : Jungle dispensary

From the very start there was never a dull moment. People flocked to the dispensary in their hundreds and it was quite impossible to deal with them all during our first week. No surgery, apart from the stitching up of a few cuts, had ever been done before, and it was quite obvious that the number of operations needed for growths alone, would keep us busy for months to come, apart from any emergency surgery that needed to be done.

The existing dispensary consisted of a small, thatched mud and wattle hut where everything took place and where medicines were made up and served to the patients through an open window. An open-sided shelter nearby served as a 'waiting-room', and opposite was another simple, thatched hut acting as the 'ward'. The windows had wooden shutters and there was a narrow doorway. The floor was simply hard mud, which, when and if swept, produced a cloud of dust which successfully covered everyone and everything within range! There were twelve roughly made wooden beds upon which were raffia mats serving as mattresses. A few rough tables were scattered here and there; people had to be in homelike surroundings or they just pined away. They would pull the shutters over the windows so that there was hardly a breath of air. The dirtier and darker the surroundings, the quicker they seemed to improve, if they were going to improve at all. Not only did the patient occupy his or her allocated space, but all the attending relatives and friends piled in too. Frequently, two or three people would be on the bed whilst the patient lay on a mat on the floor; a mutual agreement presumably, but somewhat disconcerting when you were trying to sort out which one was the patient!

There were rough huts or shelters in the compound where friends and relatives were supposed to stay and where they cooked the patients' meals, amidst a muddle of pots, baskets, chickens, goats and dogs.

To adjust from the immaculate and well ordered wards in which we had been trained, with their cleanliness, sterility, fresh air, modern facilities and equipment, to these conditions was not easy, but at this stage we had to gain the confidence of the people, so we could only accept their way of life and hope to improve the situation by the time we established the hospital.

There was, of course, no electricity, running water, plumbing or air-conditioning, no oxygen or blood transfusing. Mosquitoes and flies of every variety swarmed in the atmosphere. The ward was constantly hot and stuffy, to say nothing of the smell; a mixture of unwashed bodies and kwanga (a horrid-smelling African bread made from manioc, which they chewed constantly).

Most of the patients came on foot, winding their way through the narrow forest paths, sometimes from a distance of 200 kilometres, which would take them many days. Some came in dugout canoes on the nearby river, some propped up on a bicycle or a pick-a-back. Occasionally, patients arrived in the back of a lorry, bouncing and bumping along the rough mud road, which ended in nothing more than a track as they neared the mission. They made up a curious, mixed crowd. They arrived with their families, baskets of food, cook pots and water gourds; many brought their dogs, chickens and goats too. If they were too ill to walk, relatives and friends carried them in a hammock made of liana (forest vine) strips slung on bamboo poles. The people were mainly from the local tribes but, as word got round, many came from more distant tribes with different dialects, which made diagnosis very complicated. There was no other medical work at all within a radius of at least 200 kilometres.

We often thought longingly of the smart, white ambulance at home, rushing through smooth, crowded streets with an emergency, to a hospital geared for action, nurses ready, a doctor on call, emergencies dealt with in a matter of hours and every facility available for every situation; how different it was here. Maybe it was a flashback to scenes of the bamboo ambulance arriving that inspired us to inaugurate the ECHO project of jungle ambulances converted from renovated landrovers. What a wonderful blessing these ambulances were to so many isolated concerns.

By 7 a.m. each morning people packed the 'waiting room' and milled around the dispensary, holding high-pitched conversations under the shady trees; a seething mass of humanity, all desperately in need of some kind of medical attention. We would examine patients all day and often have to send as many as two hundred away. They would come back the next day, together with many more.

'What's the matter with you?'

'I have a little 'nyama' (animal) inside me', is the vague reply.

'But where is the pain?'

'It starts here and goes t-e-e-e-e-e to there', is the vivid description! These people often 'hurt' everywhere they were touched, just to convince us that this was 'Mpasi mingi mpenge' ('very big pain', meaning that they really were sick)!

Diagnosis was not easy with such inadequate help and so many languages to interpret. I remember one patient who was convinced that his heart had dropped; another just could not understand why, when complaining of pain in his head, was given medicine to put in his tummy! The stethoscope was a constant source of amazement, and anyone missing out a turn of having his 'organs' tuned in, was most upset. Some considered it of the utmost importance to have a pair of spectacles, whether they needed them or not. It didn't really matter whether there was any glass in the frames, for they only wanted them to improve their looks; they felt more distinguished!

Dental treatment was no problem; two pairs of ancient forceps, the patient in a chair, head held by a helper, a pull and a twist and out came the offending molar. Today, dental forceps and equipment are very much part of ECHO's distribution service.

Medicines had to be administered with care, to ensure that only essentials were given. We had very few compared with the need. It was not unknown for a patient to spit up his pill when no-one was looking and sell it in the village as 'powerful white man's medicine', regardless of what the pill had been administered for!

Within a week or two we had our first strangulated hernia. He arrived in a raffia mat sling looking very ill and was obviously in great pain. By means of signs and interpretation, we managed to find out that he had been carried through the forest for five days; we would need to operate. During these early days, the only operating instruments we had consisted of one scalpel, a pair of scissors, a roll of anatomy instruments last used in the dissecting rooms of Edinburgh University on a cadaver!, a pair of rubber gloves, towels, two operating gowns and a wooden table. We knew that the man would die if he was left, so we decided to operate with what we had, plus a darning needle, some ordinary sewing thread and palm fibre that would do for strong outer stitches. All the instruments, etc., had to be boiled up on the cook house stove to make them as sterile as possible; there was no other way. Fortunately, we had a little anaesthetic so we got to work repairing the hernia, using our improvised equipment to the best of our ability. Throughout the operation the relatives wailed and threw dust over their bodies, assuming that the patient would die anyway. The situation was not improved by the inadequate light from our hurricane lantern, which was a central meeting place for hundreds of insects, many falling on the operating site from time to time! Fortunately, we had an ampoule of penicillin (new in those early days) to counteract any ill effects from our lack of sterility. The operation was completed and almost immediately our patient showed signs of improvement. What a thrill it was to assure the relatives that this man would not die now. We charged one duck for this operation!

Our first surgical case at Yuli survived and to the day we left, every time we passed through his village he would rush out of his hut and present us with a cabbage, a chicken, a bunch of bananas or a bundle of onions; he was so grateful.

Of course, we had to let the crowds 'look in' on what we were doing in the dispensary in order to gain their confidence. The windows were covered with mosquito netting instead of glass, really to allow any breeze there was to refresh us, and also to keep out the insects, but there was always a constant sea of black faces watching us through the netting. With the normal hot humidity of a tropical day combined with the odour of a crowd of unwashed bodies, as well as the lack of light and fresh air, work became very difficult. When it was unbearable and the people failed to respond to our plea for more light and air, we posted a nurse near the window with an ear syringe full of water. This he periodically aimed at the sea of faces and pressed the plunger! It was amidst an uproar that the faces scattered and for a brief spell we were able to breath again before the next performance.

On the whole the patients were really appreciative of what we were trying to do, although our work was constantly being hampered by the lack of drugs, dressings and equipment. Although we could not understand it at the time, our Heavenly Father was taking us through a period of invaluable experience for the work He was preparing us to do through ECHO in later years. These simple conditions, lack of facilities, equipment and drugs, were imprinted upon our minds to such an extent that in years to come we were burdened and constrained to do something constructive to alleviate a situation which was not just restricted to Africa.

The 'magic needle' injection which we used in numerous cases, worked wonders and was very popular. In gratitude, the people would arrive with chickens, occasionally a duck, dried meat or fish, arrows, spears, coins, a bowl of grain or even a goat.

They came, day after day, often two hundred outpatients in one day. We saw many in need of surgery but, apart from desperate emergencies when we did what we could with what we had, we would have to send them away to return later, when we hoped to have more equipment to deal with them. Some of those patients never did return, but died in their villages.

Children were often terrified, for many had never seen a white man before. The babies, still on the breast (a process which lasted for two years) were fat and chubby and had velvety skins, but they were constantly in contact with infection of all kinds and, when they came off the breast, they were expected to plunge straight into an adult diet which was generally heavy and highly seasoned. It was at this stage that they were most vulnerable. I remember one child with a haemoglobin of 18% because of hookworm infestation, and babies who were desperately ill with severe cases of measles, pneumonia or amoebic dysentery; children thin and emaciated and infested with parasites. Many of these little ones had been treated by the Medicine man until the parents, in desperation, had trekked miles through the forest to try the new 'white medicine man' about whom they had heard. Often there was little we could do at this stage; they were too far gone for treatment.

Living in a constantly hot, humid and damp atmosphere, many people came to us with respiratory conditions such as pneumonia, tuberculosis, pleurisy, bronchitis and whooping cough.

Insects cause the spread of many tropical diseases. Sleeping sickness results from the sting of the tsetse fly and, in those days, killed many. Malaria is transmitted by a species of mosquito and, if neglected, blackwater fever develops, followed almost certainly by death.

We were constantly up against the problem of worms; hookworms, roundworms, micro-filaires which often produced elephantiasis, with greatly swollen organs and limbs. Onchoceriasis, or river blindness, is transmitted by the simulium damnosum or 'Black fly'. This disease often remains dormant for some years before giving rise to symptoms. Sometimes a patient suffering from an infestation of worms was treated by the Medicine man in the village, with serious consequences. The jigger is a sand flea which causes no problem if treated quickly, the tiny sac of eggs being easily removed from under the toe nail, but if left untreated, can cause ulceration and even the loss of a toe. We saw many cases of scabies, as well as unpleasant effects from a variety of other insects such as leeches, spiders, centipedes, scorpions, ants, ticks, bugs, lice and fleas. Snakes bites, too, from certain species caused alarming symptoms which were often fatal. How difficult it was to diagnose the extent of the damage in these cases without a microscope or facilities to examine blood. The ECHO Alpha microscope revolutionised the situation in this field of medicine. Other common problems were tropical ulcers, poliomyelitis, Congo red fever, (transmitted when the urine of infested rats contaminates food or kitchen utensils), and yaws, resulting from inadequate sanitation and cleanliness. Smallpox was not uncommon; the people were suspicious of vaccination and often interfered by rubbing earth into the scar, which occasionally resulted in fatal tetanus. In any case, it was most difficult to obtain vaccine and, when we did, we had no refrigerator in which to keep it. Leprosy was seen almost daily, but in those early days we had very few facilities or drugs for treatment. There were many other types of cases that crowded daily into the dispensary such as influenza, rheumatism, mumps, meningitis, lumbago and the occasional case of typhus or relapsing fever. Malnutrition was very prevalent with inadequate diets, resulting in cases of severe anaemia and other complications.

There were always a number of common abscesses to incise, but the nurses were able to deal with these. Again, there was the problem of not having adequate supplies of antibiotics to cope with the vast number of needy cases.

Interruptions were routine; accident cases arrived and had to receive immediate attention. One baby had extensive burns after falling into the fire; knife and spear wounds often to be cleaned and stitched up, or fish bones stuck in the throat; men fallen out of palm trees; gaping wounds caused by animals such as leopards, hippos, elephants or crocodiles, women who had spilt boiling oil over their arms. These were very difficult days filled with humbling experiences. How often we longed for civilised aids and conditions. With the heat and the insects, the constant demand made upon us, and the medley of languages to interpret, we sometimes wondered why we were there at all. All too often the missionary call is glamorised beyond reality. The heroic send-off, the exciting journey and new experiences were followed by a return to earth with a severe bump and a shattering shake-up. We had to serve suffering humanity, knowing what to do, but being unable to do it because it was either too late or what was needed to alleviate the situation was not available. It was even hard to pray; how much we needed the daily power of the Holy Spirit to enable us to bring a ray of hope to these people whom God had entrusted to our care.

Life goes on, whether in the heart of Africa or in the middle of Europe and here in the forest babies were born just the same. Girls were brought up from an early age to work hard in the gardens, and were used to carrying heavy baskets on their backs, so the pelvis tended to become wide and the ligaments supple, which naturally prepared them for childbirth. Birth was no mystery to them, but a natural occurrence. An African woman who could not bear children had a real problem and she was looked upon in disgust.

In her natural environment, a woman would go into the forest to have her baby, making a little clearing where she would hide; like an animal, she must be alone. Often interference by the Medicine man in a case of difficulty, led to death, sometimes of both mother and child.

It was terrible having to deliver babies in squalid conditions after the luxury of modern facilities at home, but we had to do what we could with what we had. Sometimes a baby would be born before we could reach the hut, or we were not called on time. There it would be, lying naked and cold on a leaf on the ground, whilst mother and grandmother would be quite indifferent to the immediate needs of the newly born. We tried to encourage the pregnant women to come to welfare clinics and in this way we were able to treat any parasitic conditions, check the development of the baby and try to give advice where it would be accepted, but this was not easy and often a woman had some kind of fetish or charm fixed under her breast to promote milk supply or for some other superstitious belief. Sometimes it was too late to do anything for a ruptured uterus following prolonged labour or to perform a Caesarean section, for which we had not got the necessary instruments.

We had hardly been at Yuli more than a few hours, when cries and wails were heard in the direction of the little maternity ward, and we all rushed down to be confronted by our first desperate emergency. This was a case of obstructed labour and the baby was already dead in utero. There was absolutely nothing we could do but rapidly to carry out a destructive operation and complete the delivery of the dead baby in order to save the life of the mother. We made an instrument out of a bucket handle in order to carry out a craniotomy. It was a horrific experience, especially as the whole thing had to be done by the light of a flickering paraffin lamp, which cast weird shadows and made everything very eerie and even more shocking. Of course, this wasn't helped by the frenzied cries and wails of the relatives.

It was the practise of relatives to remove a patient during the night if they thought death was near. This happened time and time again, when probably if left to complete treatment, the patient would have recovered. But these people felt very strongly that death should take place in their own environments; it was something to do with the spirits. It seemed that they would try to prolong life if they could. In the village all the relatives were called together and they crowded into the tiny hut of the sick man. They called to him and talked to him and gave him no rest at all, even throwing cold water over him if he tried to sleep! When there was a death, the wailing of the relatives and friends was a fearsome thing; they wailed themselves hoarse to prove that they were not responsible for the death.

Wailing reached a crescendo as the grave was reached, but after it was all over, they would relax and make merry, dancing and feasting. The drums beat out their messages to the villages around and everyone seemed to have a good time.

The people came in their hundreds and thousands during those early months. It was heartbreaking to see some of the cases for whom we could so often do so little, either because the disease had been left too long, because of delay by long distances, or because of involvement with village medicine, but more often than not, because we had not got the tools for the job. I continue to emphasise this point because I am convinced that the Lord was already preparing our concerns for the desperate needs everywhere in the Third World for medical help.

We started courses of lectures and introduced some of the girls to ward techniques and simple treatments; it was quite unnatural for them to look after sick people other than close relatives. The two African male nurses, however, learnt quickly and we were soon able to leave a considerable amount of responsibility with them; sorting out record cards, dealing with the dressing of wounds and ulcers and making up simple medicines. They were able to give intravenous injections, making gland or spinal punctures or pull teeth. Later, we taught them the techniques of surgery and giving of anaesthetics. They had to see and feel the ideas they retained; their educational background was so entirely different from ours that it was hard to evaluate their ability properly.

Life went on, day after day, week after week, in the little dispensary, with the never-ending stream of patients and all the other numerous tasks that had to be attended to: administration work, government reports, salaries of workers, drug orders, medical finance, preparation of building materials for the new hospital, upkeep and maintenance of property and grounds, surplus food to distribute, family responsibilities, preparation of sermons, time for fellowship and prayer with our two colleagues, and a hundred and one other details. Often during those early days we felt near to despair and exhaustion.

The conditions under which we were working were enough to shock the most adaptable of people, but we had no alternative. We had been sent out to create a simple hospital from all this and our determined natures were not to be put off; create a simple hospital we would.

....oOo....

6 : Creating a hospital

The first Congo hospital was created at Boma in 1889, followed ten years later by the first laboratory at Leopoldville. Belgium was anxious to improve the living conditions of the Congolese people, so later on, a Welfare Fund was created. A grant of £1,000 was allocated at Yuli, which meant that we were able to obtain a basic stock of new medical equipment and drugs for the new hospital. A small Bedford van was also donated through the Memorial Hospital Fund. But since the coming of Independence in 1960, the annual grant stopped.

Before we arrived, the building of a Memorial Hospital had actually started, under the supervision of Nellie Hadaway, who had begun the original work at Yuli. She had worked together with Elsie Saunders for the past few years, looking after the dispensary, school, church and district work. Their wisdom and guidance was invaluable as we settled down to the situation at Yuli.

Bricks for the hospital buildings were made from anthill clay, which was puddled by the brickmakers' feet, then pressed by hand into wooden brick moulds and laid out to dry in the sun before being carefully stacked into a kiln. Sand was collected from the river and timber felled in the forest.

Daily, amidst his other activities, James had to supervise the building work, urging on the various squads of workmen. We were anxious to get the theatre finished first so that we could start operating on the fast-growing list of waiting cases.

The theatre contained three rooms: the operating room; a store, dispensary and 'scrubbing up' room; and a room for sterilising and cleaning instruments, etc. The windows were low and covered with mosquito gauze. This would enable people outside to see what was going on; thus we would have a better opportunity to gain their confidence.

We had to collect the first crates of equipment from a staging post on the river, which involved a journey through the forest swamps in a huge dugout canoe. The landing stage was merely a rough platform jutting down

'A jungle operating theatre

to the river edge, with a small group of mud houses and a few fishing huts. As the task of loading began, the first box bounced its way across the landing stage, assisted by willing hands. At the edge, other hands took over, as some of the men standing in the canoe waited to receive it. Amidst a deafening deluge of loud utterances, the box precariously changed hands and finished up with a loud thud as the canoe handlers underestimated its weight. Other boxes followed suit. Then came a large drum. By this time the pace had hotted up and the usual display of African drama had entered the scene. This particular drum seemed to be affected in quite the wrong way as it suddenly took off from the cluster of greasy hands and rolled gaily across the stage on its own with a host of shrieking men in hot pursuit.

'Stop it,' yelled James in anguish, but his cries were in vain. The drum continued its roll, oblivious of all the drama, did a little hiccup on the edge of the platform and then fell with a loud 'plop' into the water below. En route, however, it created some havoc. One fellow whose arms were stretched out to catch it, was completely ignored as the drum skimmed across his head and hit the next man a broadsider. He, without argument, gracefully toppled over the edge of the canoe to accompany the drum into the muddy water of the river!

Finally, the last box was positioned and we were ready to depart. With the usual commotion, chatter and farewells, we pulled away from the stage on our homeward journey.

This first consignment of equipment meant so much to us and we praised the Lord for His bountiful provision and for the folk involved on the giving end. There were glass cupboards, trolleys, ward equipment, a simple operating table, instruments, etc. It was great fun now, furnishing the first hospital block - the theatre. Later on more equipment would arrive, more instruments for the theatre and beds, etc., for the wards. But now we had enough to start on a long list of the smaller operations, once the theatre was officially opened.

The day after the opening we started. The low mosquito gauze windows enabled the people to see everything that was going on; the windows were packed with curious faces and there was hardly a sound. A spinal anaesthetic meant that the patient was conscious and, as we slipped the knife neatly across the abdomen, you could literally hear a unanimous gasp, as the people tried to fathom out why the patient did not leap off the table with terrified yells of agony!

During the daily programme, now divided between the dispensary and the theatre, time had to be allowed for supervision of the next hospital building which was to be a new ward. James had to whip off his operating gown, gloves and mask and go outside, climb up the rough scaffolding and check on the levels or supervise the construction of another brick kiln. He would then make his way back to the operating theatre to start on the next case.

The days were not without their dramas and frustrations. If the door of the operating theatre was accidentally left open, it was a ready access for goats, ducks, chicken or dogs. It did not help to have a goat suddenly butting into your posterior, or a chicken flapping feathers around the 'sterile' site!

Quite often we had to resort to a large surgical atlas that we had brought out with us from England. If it was a case with which James was unfamiliar, there being no consultant to turn to, he would rely on me reading the next step from the atlas propped at the foot of the operating table.

The most common routine operation cases were strangulated hernias, fibroids, ovarian cysts, tumours, fractures and cataracts. Blind people came from far and wide, and the many who had a straightforward cataract, to remove the opaque lens was dramatic and miraculous magic to them. Payment for the operations varied according to the status of the patient;

often it was in kind, such as a goat, chicken, duck or eggs.

It was not unusual to spend long hours operating on a case, with apparent success, only to discover that during the night a relative had entered the ward to give a dose of violent native medicine, just in case the white doctor's medicine did not work, or sometimes to remove the patient altogether!

There were, however, one or two spectacular cases that we will never forget.

'Everything is ready, doctor' called Efoma, as we approached the theatre one morning to start an operation session. Today, we were to repair the hernia of a local Chief. A quick check to be quite certain we had all that we needed, then we were ready to begin. The operating table that had been sent was a very simple one, with no special attachments, but it was an improvement on the wooden table set-up we had used previously.

The Chief, draped in towels, lay smiling up with an expression of satisfaction. To say the least, he was enormous; eighteen stone of Chief literally overlapping the flimsy operating table on both sides, while the towels camouflaged the huge mound of his abdomen. We sat him up to give him a spinal anaesthetic; it was at this point that the drama began. He must have shifted slightly when the needle was injected into his spine but, whatever he did, there followed a tremendous crash; the table seemed to fold up as the Chief, draped in green towels, slid gracefully on to the floor; he landed with a resounding thud! We had actually injected 'heavy' procaine into his spinal canal which, as he sat up, should have 'sunk' down the spine to anaesthetise the lower part of his anatomy. If he was left lying on the floor for many seconds, the procaine might easily go in the wrong direction, with disastrous effects on the brain!

In the midst of this fiasco, the instrument trolley skidded across the floor and somehow got entangled with the sliding Chief, sending dishes, instruments and catgut in all directions. One nurse let out a yell as an abdominal retractor caught him between the eyes, and faces scattered from the gauze windows as a shower of artery forceps, scissors and scalpels hurtled towards them! People from all directions rushed to our aid; sterility was completely unobserved as the roaring Chief was rapidly hoisted into an upright position and then lifted back on to the table which, this time, was being firmly anchored by various people.

Once order had been restored, we rapidly re-sterilised ourselves and our equipment, for we had no spare instruments to replace those that had been originally set up. The first incision was made and then it was just a question of ploughing our way through layer upon layer of fat, and when we got down into the depths of all this, we had to 'negotiate' our way along the true abdominal wall to find the hernia. It was a great moment when we reached this stage and, as we almost elbowed the fat back from the site, the repair was successfully carried out and the layers of fat returned. It was a great relief to get the Chief on to a bed in a section of the little ward, with all his retinue and wives dancing attendance upon him to fulfil his every need.

As we were checking some ward cases one evening, we heard a commotion outside the dispensary. Dozens of people were chattering and yelling at one another, more concerned with sorting out their palaver than showing concern for their patient, who had been wounded in their tribal fight. His wrist and forearm were broken and his skull badly crushed; there was considerable blood loss and no means of blood transfusing. This repair job took many hours as we worked on his brain, repairing membranes and removing clots and then fitting many pieces of broken bones together. This was not the easiest of tasks under the light of a pressure lamp and the occasional help of a torch. We required much patience, too, as we sutured the torn tendons in the wrist and set the arm in plaster.

Nine months later, a man arrived at the outpatients clinic, hurling a stream of complaints at James and pointing to his head. Suddenly, we remembered that this was the man with whom we had spent many hours in an attempt to save his life. On examination, we found that the many pieces of smashed skull had healed beautifully, and the hand and arm were in perfect working order. But he was complaining about a slight bump on his head!

James looked thoughtful.

'Inginda,' he called to one of the nurses, 'bring me a machete. I want to return this man's skull to what it was like before the operation.'

As he turned to instruct the patient to go into the examination room, there was no-one there; we saw him disappearing down the dispensary path at the rate of knots, never to return again!

Inginda and I were halfway through mixing up a gallon of 'mist.expect.' one morning, when we heard the familiar commotion of an advancing emergency. The man in command bellowed a vivid description of the accident case, waving his arms dramatically as he chattered on in the dialect of his tribe. The patient was a palm nut cutter who had, apparently, slipped and fallen twenty feet from the top of a palm tree to the ground below; he had broken his leg. We had no x-ray to diagnose the exact position of the broken bones, so we just manipulated the bones into an approximately correct position by 'feeling' for the broken pieces.

We made the plaster extra thick so that there was no risk of the mended fracture breaking down. The relatives could not understand why we wanted to keep him in for two months after the plaster had been applied; after all, they figured, we had given him a new and stronger leg, so what was there to wait for? We tried to explain that he would not be keeping the plaster on for ever, but they could not get the point. If he had stayed in the village, the medicine man would probably have buried the leg in earth and then lit a fire over the fractured area.

This was something we were constantly up against. Patients were reasonably happy to stay in the hospital if something was being done regularly, like a dressing or injections or daily doses of medicine, but they could not tolerate simple rest cures.

So it was that a couple weeks later our patient vanished! We immediately sent out search parties in various directions to try and find a man with a plaster leg hobbling through the forest; we never did track him down.

Having tackled some of the smaller operations first, in order to gain the confidence of the people, we now felt the time had come to attempt some of the more complicated tumours awaiting surgery. We had received a further small supply of equipment from England which relieved the situation considerably, although still left much to be desired. Our first really big tumour was a pelvic growth. With very few artery forceps and no plasma or blood, we worked carefully on until at last the mass was removed. As usual, many morbid faces lined the window, and uttered awed moans to one another as the operation progressed. As was our custom, one nurse was allocated to take 'the lump' round to the waiting crowds so that they could see exactly what had been removed! This was the 'evil' that had been extracted from within the patient. Once again the white man's magic had worked a miracle in the eyes of the people, and they rejoiced at the wonder of it all. Our responsibilities were very considerable, and how thrilling it was to be able to tell the people that our skill was only helping them because the Great Physician Himself had enabled us to be trained and sent to their aid.

We removed another enormous growth from a woman who had a facial elephantiasis. The growth had gradually increased in size and at the time of the operation it weighed 20 pounds. The left eye was four inches under a skin flap and the growth dropped to her waistline. She complained that it got in the way when she was trying to sleep! This was a very difficult operation and in the middle she collapsed, and we had to stop everything to resuscitate her before we could continue. Finally, the task was completed and with the mass removed, her face took on a more normal appearance.

We had just finished supper one evening and were sitting quietly back reminiscing on the activities of the day. It was very hot and oppressive and the air was very still and quiet. Efoma came puffing up the steps on to the back veranda of our house.

'Can you come at once, doctor,' he panted. 'We have a man who has been eaten by a hippo.'

We had visions of the chewed remains of a corpse as we collected our hurricanes and made our way down the familiar path to the dispensary. A wind was getting up now and we could hear it thundering its way through the forest tree-tops. As we neared the hospital compound, doors and windows were beginning to bang and a plastic bucket took off, flying wildly past us up the path.

We quickly took cover in the little dispensary, where the mangled body of a man lay on an improvised stretcher, surrounded by sobbing relatives and friends; this was a local fisherman. He had been out fishing at dusk apparently, and had paddled too close to a mother hippo with her young offspring. In a protective rage and with a mighty roar, the mother hippo had opened her vast mouth and upset the flimsy canoe, tipping the terrified fisherman into the water.

The storm was now gathering momentum; isolated trees bent and twisted and the hurricane lamps kept blowing out. Part of the dispensary roof was torn off and a deluge descended beside the examining table where our patient lay. We covered him with a plastic sheet and made a frantic dash to the operating theatre. The rain ran down our necks, our feet were soaked in minutes and we were almost airborne by the wind. It was hopeless to attempt complete sterility, so we didn't try. Thunder and lightning followed continuously with startling suddenness, as we commenced the biggest sewing job we had yet tackled. Miraculously, there were no broken bones, but the torn flesh in the man's back involved 86 stitches. It wasn't easy to see what we were doing, and the lights we did have swayed backwards and forwards, despite shutters over the windows, so that shadows were cast and weird patterns formed across the room.

Then, as suddenly as it had come, the storm passed away and there was calm once more. Some thatch had been blown off the ward, and an array of buckets adorned the floor. The beds were covered in bits from the thatch but, despite the circumstances, we praised the Lord that we had been able to help yet another of His children in distress.

One of the most dramatic operations we performed was on a woman who had suddenly been taken with acute abdominal pain. She lived in a riverside village and relatives, knowing of the white doctor's magic, bundled her into a canoe and brought her to Yuli. She was almost pulseless from a massive internal haemorrhage caused by a ruptured ectopic pregnancy. The woman was going to need blood and, as usual, we hadn't got any. No African would offer blood; it was against their tribal customs. Most of them were so full of parasites and infection that it would not be safe to use anyway.

James considered that if we slipped a surgical trocar through the abdominal wall into the free haemorrhage, collected and citrated the blood to prevent it clotting, we could then drip it back into the collapsed veins of the patient as the emergency operation was commenced. This proved to be a brilliant idea and worked wonderfully well. To our great delight she recovered and, once again, we had been able to prove that in the strength and wisdom of God the seemingly impossible task had proved successful, and a life had been saved by a very unorthodox medical procedure. It never ceased to amaze us what we could do when we had to, without modern facilities.

Perhaps the most widely publicised case in the district involved the local Chief's wife, whose babies had all died because, we discovered, she had a deformed pelvis. In desperation the Chief agreed to let us operate on her this time, providing we produced a son for him. To think that we could 'kill' the mother, produce a live baby (caesarean section) and then bring the mother back to life!

'It's a boy!' exclaimed James, to the tense crowds, 'and he is quite well and healthy.'

The people started yelling and shouting with joy.

'It's a son; the Chief has a son!'

Word spread fast from village to village, and in no time at all, people appeared from the nearby villages to join in the celebrations. The Chief, dressed in wild cat and monkey skins, with neck, ankles and arms decorated with leopards' teeth and coloured beads, was overjoyed and greeted us with a tremendous grin of satisfaction, his white teeth glistening between his thick lips. Most of that night the celebrations continued; dancing is a vital part of African life, and plays a major role at a time like this.

It was not rare for a mother to give birth to twins, but in many of the tribes it was thought to be a bad omen and often, back in the isolated villages, the babies would be left to die in the forest.

Mama Esengo came to Yuli for her confinement. She had a difficult delivery, but two babies eventually arrived safely. It was then that we realised that nature's task was not complete, and a third baby was on its way! Fortunately, this was a sensible couple who lived near to the mission and we were able to persuade them to ignore any superstition presented to them by the local medicine man. For many months we supplemented the babies' feeds with powdered milk, and then helped the mother to wean them properly. They grew into three healthy little girls and were the centre of attraction and admiration, the first set of triplets ever to be born and reared in our area.

And so, week by week we tackled an increasing list of surgical cases, with the minimum of equipment and inadequate facilities. But when God calls, He equips and gives knowledge and skill. Now, as we look back we are so grateful for the experience we gained during those years in Africa, resulting in a real understanding of some of the many difficulties medical personnel have to face in such remote areas.

....oOo....

7 : Through the valley of clouds

But we were not without our own medical problems. One day James had to go down to the landing stage to collect materials for the new hospital buildings. As he was loading up the canoe, a scorpion got into his shorts and stung him in three places before he discovered it. Anyone who has had experience with scorpions will know how dangerous one sting can be. Great weals showed up at the sites of the stings, then swelling, partially relieved by adrenaline injections, spread to his face, until his eyes were quite hidden and his lips puffed up so that he could hardly move his mouth. Then his throat began to close and he begged me to do a tracheotomy; I just hung on to the syringe and prayed the swelling down as an alternative! It worked, praise the Lord!

Then, on another occasion, James had an infected bronchial cyst which needed to be incised. He gave me a scalpel. Could you cut your husband's throat! No, neither could I! So, finally he decided to incise the cyst himself, standing in front of a mirror. There were times when I felt such a coward, and these were two of the occasions.

Our first child, Josephine, was born at an American Mission Hospital, 300 kilometres away from our isolated mission station. She was two weeks late, 5 lbs in weight and a forceps delivery by the light of a hurricane lamp; there was no baby incubator for resuscitation.

Great was the rejoicing when we returned to Yuli; Josephine was the first white baby many people had ever seen in this primitive area of the Congo, and they were full of admiration expressed in an odd collection of extraordinary exclamations.

But very soon complications set in and a persistent haemorrhage involved a return to the American Mission Hospital. I have travelled in some strange vehicles in my time, but never lying flat on a mattress in the back of a borrowed lorry with a roughly made canopy of forest foliage! This was to be my ambulance.

Several operations failed, mainly through lack of equipment, and because of further complications, we sold up most of our belongings in order to finance our return flight to England for further emergency surgery. There had been a serious financial crises in the mission at home and, in those days, the missionaries used to take the brunt! We were very young and inexperienced and it was hard to accept this situation. We did not understand God's motive in this but we had no alternative. We had not anticipated this kind of problem; we had settled into our work and were thrilled to be creating a medical work in this area. It was not free of difficulties; nothing worthwhile ever is, but we were able to cope and the Lord was rewarding us with wonderful blessings. Now we had come to a point when we just had to hand over to Him and accept the situation as it was.

Back home, a long hospital spell resulted in two further operations before healing began to take place and I began to know the touch of God's hand upon me, as I returned to my normal vibrant self once more. A second daughter, Rosemary, was born while we were at home and then, as a family, two years later we returned to the Congo.

On our return to Africa, we went under the auspices of the Baptist Missionary Society to Tondo, a station which used to be run by one of the American Missions. It was situated on the shores of Lac Tumba which was 50 miles long and 10 miles across. We were 150 kilometres from the nearest town of Coquilhatville.

Our house was similar to the one at Yuli except here we had ceilings on the rooms and water in the house, which came from a series of petrol drums set up as a water system outside the 'bathroom'; we were living in luxury!

As we settled down to our daily routine, I found my work now had to be geared to the children and I spent little time on the medical team. I needed to be with them as much as possible, so they joined me at the sewing classes and a weekly Bible group. Also I took them round the station as I supervised 200 schoolboys working on the gardening and tidying programmes, and the able-bodied leprosy patients on their work programme. As the children grew, they joined the Sunday School and, later, attended the daily kindergarten classes. Home was a firm base and we always made a lot of birthday celebrations and events such as Christmas, with parties and other festivities. But priority was given to the real meaning of Christmas and the children joined the celebrations in the church, which was always decorated with tropical flowers.

But it is no joke bringing up a family in the middle of the African jungle. The children kept remarkably fit on the whole, despite their constant contact with disease and often unhygienic conditions. An African woman helped to look after them while we were busy, and they learnt many African ways and games as they played with their little African friends, chattering far more in the Bantu dialect than in English. One morning we found a huge centipede in Josephine's dolly pram. How good the Lord was to show us before she saw it. Almost certainly she would have picked it up, and a sting from a centipede could have proved fatal to a three-year-old. Time and time again we proved the goodness and protection of the Lord in these situations. We made a little miniature mud and wattle house for them, and hours of fun were spent here.

Josephine and Rosemary with their African friends

A picnic on 'sandy beach' was an outing we treated ourselves to on occasions when we were free to get away for an hour or two. We used to pack into the big canoe which had an outboard motor, and the children thought it was a great idea. 'Sandy beach' was a delightfully secluded spot, under the shade of forest and palm trees, the water of the lake gently lapping on the silver sand; an excellent place to bathe and play and have a picnic.

On one occasion, the outboard motor refused to ignite when we were ready to return; we just had to row and make a noise to ward off any hippos or crocodiles around, and hug the coast to make sure we were on the right course. As the daylight faded, the moon rose over the lake and gave us enough light to see where we were going. How relieved we were when our missionary mechanic came to look for us; he soon started the motor and we were on our way.

After two years, we set off on a mid-term holiday, to visit the eastern area of the Congo bordering on Uganda. We took our car on the large, passenger river boat to Stanleyville, then headed for the mountains of Rwanda, travelling during the day, stopping by night at mission stations or state posts en route. Unfortunately, both children contracted measles (at different times) along the way, which rather threw our schedule out of order. Nevertheless, we visited the game parks of East Africa and the pygmy area in the Epulu forest. We bathed in the waters of Lake Kivu and climbed the lower heights of Mt. Rwanzori. Returning to our station we drove along rough forest roads, often being stopped by huge forest trees blown down during a storm. We covered 5,000 miles and returned to our work refreshed and reinvigorated to take up our tasks once more. I often wonder how much our two daughters, now married, remember about that wonderful tour.

Jungle hospital cook house and ward

There was an established hospital work at Tondo, so we found things much less primitive than we had been accustomed to - still, of course, with much to be desired. The hospital day started at 6 a.m., as the station drum sounded out, to call the staff to morning prayers before the routine of the day. Later, some 300 outpatients gathered for the morning Gospel service. For some of these people from far away villages, this message was new, a message of life and salvation.

One of our nurses

Then the work programme began and the outpatients were sorted out for treatment. Here at Tondo there was more help from the African nurses, which gave James more time to concentrate on the ever-growing operation list. He also had two other European nurses to work with him. There was always a hub of activity in the outpatients' department, and babies being delivered in the maternity unit. There were routine ward rounds and constant interruptions when an emergency arrived, sometimes needing immediate surgery. There were lectures to fit in and villages clinics to visit, apart from the vast amount of office work needing attention.

There was a small leprosy colony near to the hospital compound. This was set up by Dr. Alfred Russell, who served for many years at Tondo. A small chapel was erected in the grounds in memory of his daughter, who died in 1943. Services were regularly held here and many patients were blessed through the ministry of the Word.

Leprosy is not the dreaded disease it used to be and James had the joy of being one of the first doctors to use Dapsone, the wonder drug for the cure of leprosy. In those days we did not visualise the time when, through ECHO, 200 million Dapsone tablets would be sent out to all parts of the world in one year. Today, many patients need not stay in hospital for treatment if they are diagnosed in the early stages; excellent results and cures are now being obtained by the administration of this, combined with other more recent drugs.

Each Sunday in the open-sided chapel the lepers had their own worship service. The people came, crippled or active, clothed or unclothed. They sang their hearts out in a most untuneful manner, but the Lord would not object to that; at least they were making a joyful noise! Many came to know Jesus, the Great Physician Himself; then, although disfigured and maimed, they experienced great joy, and endeavoured to witness and share their joy with others. How wonderful to know that one day they will be like Him and see Him face to face; they will have no disfigurement then, but new and perfect bodies.

Nsombele had been an unwanted sufferer of leprosy. She arrived at the mission in a state of exhaustion; her hands and feet were stumps and her face was distorted. She became a Christian soon after her arrival and was a great intercessor and evangelist, introducing many a needy soul to the Saviour. Her radiant face mirrored the light and joy and peace in her soul. Now, Nsombele is rid of her poor diseased body, happy to be in the place prepared for her, at home with her Lord.

Some medical trips involved crossing the lake. On one particular occasion, when James left with one of the nurses and a couple of helpers, they had quite an experience. A few miles out from the shore, a threatening storm overtook them and they had a pretty rough time as waves, lashed by the wind into a fury, crashed against the canoe, breaking in a soaking deluge over the occupants. The lake was invisible beyond a curtain of pelting rain but, eventually, almost at the end of their tether, the dripping stalwarts were driven on to a narrow, rocky peninsula. Here they discovered the saucer-like footprints of a hippo trail in the mud and, by following it, they eventually reached the forest road. It was just by chance that a Company truck was passing that way and gladly picked up the weary travellers and took them back to the mission. Once more, there was cause to rejoice, as the protecting and leading hand of the Lord had been with them all the way.

From time to time, we used to visit Coquilhatville, our nearest town 150 kilometres away. Here we could stock up with some food items and other necessities when they were available. Near to the town was the American Mission station of Bolenge and sometimes we would stay a day or two, when we were travelling in that area. They always made us welcome, and it gave us a break from the daily routine and a well appreciated rest.

I remember one occasion in particular when we visited our missionary friends, Steve and Sue, at Bolenge.

'Hi, Doc and Peggy! How are you? Good to see you. Did you have a good trip?'

'Hi! We're fine and the children have been really looking forward to our visit, but we had a bit of a shake-up at Meketi, at the narrow bridge there. One of our back wheels jammed in a rut between two rotten logs. It took us half an hour to lever it out, and that has damaged the tyre!'

'Well, I'm sure you're ready to have some lunch and freshen up, so come on.' He paused, then added, 'Oh! By the way, Doc, we have Jenny sick. We'd be glad if you could pop in and see her after lunch; would you mind?'

James had a strange feeling that this 'sickness' might not be as casual as Steve had made it out to be, and he was not happy to wait.

'Steve, do you think I ought to see her before lunch!'

Steve hunched his shoulders.

'If you think so, but she'll be OK for a while longer, I'm sure.'

James was certain about his feeling so, while I joined Sue with the children, Steve took James over to see Jenny. She was in considerable pain and her ashen face indicated, without doubt, that something serious was going on. James's examination revealed what he had already suspected - an advanced ectopic pregnancy with, by now, a considerable amount of internal bleeding.

'I'm sorry, Jenny, but this is going to involve immediate surgery.' He took her husband, Jack, to one side and explained that surgery was the only hope if her life was to be saved.

'She's lost a lot of blood already,' said James, 'so we will almost certainly need some blood. Do you know her blood group?'

It turned out that Jenny had a rather rare blood grouping and this did not make the problem any easier. There was no blood bank anywhere in those days, so James was going to rely entirely upon one of the missionaries. But, of all twelve missionaries, no-one had the right grouping. James suddenly remembered that he was of the same rare group, and he was aware that he must help in this emergency situation. Without transfusion she would certainly not survive; there was no alternative; he would have to give the necessary blood.

Jenny was taken to the European hospital in town without delay, and James went with her. By now, the news had spread round the mission station and everyone was aware of the emergency. There was some confusion at the hospital as the theatre was hastily prepared and James, without further ado, bared his arm, slipped the canulae into a vein and took two pints of his own blood and started it flowing into the patient. There was no time to delay; the room was a bit hazy, to say the least, but he must not consider his own desperate need to lie and rest for a while. He had to operate; time was running out. Thus, he committed the whole situation to the Lord as the first incision was made and the fight against life and death commenced. Soon the bleeding points were secured and the blood clots removed. Jenny's pulse began to respond again and the immediate danger was over.

'That's it,' said James in his usual cheerful way. He was still feeling a bit shaky himself, but he was so thankful that the Lord had co-ordinated our visit with this emergency.

"She'll be all right now,' he said to Jack. 'Keep her quiet and still for the next 24 hours; then she will slowly regain her strength. I'm so glad I was able to help. Now, I can do with some refreshment!' We heard the next year that Jenny had produced twins. She named one of them James! So much for English blood!

We had planned to come home on furlough in the late autumn of 1955, after three years' service but, at the last moment, the replacement doctor was unavailable and we were asked to stay on for an extra year, or until a relief could come. We had even packed for our anticipated furlough. But we were happy in our service for the Lord and were willing to carry on to provide the necessary medical help for these people.

However, during that fourth year things began to happen. The Congo was beginning to erupt with political unrest, and there were signs of threatening situations everywhere. One night, we were forced to send for an army contingent, posted some 30 kilometres away, and request protection. A wild tribal group had arrived at the station and threatened to kill all the patients and all the white people if we did not submit to their commands and requests. With our two young daughters to protect, I was scared and, for a brief moment, I lost hold of my grip on the Lord. I could relate to David's psalm. 'The enemy pursues (us) ... he makes (us) dwell in darkness ... (our) spirits grow faint within (us) ... O Lord, preserve (our lives); in your righteousness bring (us) out of trouble.' (Ps 143). The problem was eventually resolved and we praised the Lord for His protection for the patients and ourselves.

It was soon after this that a sudden heart attack, like a bolt out of the blue, made me feel that I was some kind of target. The acuteness of the pain brought me very low and again I struggled to maintain my grip on the Lord. Were these incidents attacks from the enemy, or were they chastenings from the Lord? With a scarcity of diagnostic equipment to confirm the extent of the damage, and even less facilities for treatment and recovery, I was rushed to the Government hospital, some 150 kilometres away. The hospital seemed to be run by antiquated nuns, I remember, and I felt that I should be looking after them! Diagnosis equipment and treatment here was no better than we already had, except they did make an effort to produce a somewhat crumpled ECG (electrocardiograph). We returned to our station, where I was cared for by our two nursing sisters. With the children it was not easy and as the condition did not improve and complications set in, once more I was bundled on to a plane, back to the UK and straight into hospital for further investigations and treatment.

The following months were slow and painful; I just couldn't understand why this had to be, specially as I was so young. How much I had to learn; how much I had to come to appreciate God's wisdom in the decisions He led us to make. As never before, we realised how much we needed close communication with the Lord at this time. The brightness of previous days became so overcast that we could not see through the thick storm clouds that seemed to surround us. The whole experience came as a shattering blow.

In the wake of our disappointments and anxiety, we did not realise at the time how significant all this was to be. I became bitter and frustrated and almost angry that God treated us in such a way. 'Why?' There had been years of training and a real assurance of the call of God to Africa. It had been so definite and without hesitation I knew this was where the Lord wanted me; I had no room for doubt, despite painful reaction, disapproval and opposition from my family at the time.

So, James settled into a busy National Health practise in London and, as I slowly recovered, we made the first steps towards making a temporary home in England, until the future was made clear. I took a course in journalism and had my first book published, together with a series of illustrated articles about African life. Together we edited and sound-taped our films. Then came the time when we were both able to take wide-spread missionary meetings. Thus, we were partially able to fulfil our missionary calling, and now, with my health greatly improved, we had high hopes that the next medical would give us the OK to return to Africa. But, once again, hopes were shattered.

'If you want to keep fit,' I was told by the Consultant Cardiologist, 'it would be foolish to return to such a climate.'

Why had we spent such a brief time in the land to which God called us to serve him! Years of preparation and dedication and now it all seemed to be over. But it is not for us to question God, only to be willing, despite our own misunderstanding of a situation, or our disagreement with what He seems to be saying. Obedience must follow willingness, even if one finds it hard to co-operate at the time.

'Lord,' I said, 'You have a purpose for me; You have not made me for nothing, so I trust You to reveal the meaning of all this.'

As the rest of this book reveals, our disappointment was God's appointment for a far wider ministry than we could ever hope to accomplish, had we remained on that remote station in the Congo jungle. But that experience of isolation and simplicity was very necessary to prepare us for the wider ministry to come. Don't ever consider that you have been let down by God. If you are certain that you have obeyed His call and have not held back from 'going forth', then there must be a reason when apparent disaster strikes, and you are overcome with disappointment and frustration. Wait patiently in faith and trust; His purposes will be revealed and you will no longer have cause to be wondering 'Why?'

'Be still and know that I am God.' *(Ps. 46:10)*

One reason for our departure from Africa soon revealed itself. In the summer of 1960, Congo was granted Independence by the Belgian Government. This was rapidly followed by rebellion, and chaos broke out throughout the Republic. Soon the horrors endured by missionaries of all denominations were headline stories of the National press of so many countries. Many missionaries were called to make the supreme sacrifice as they laid down their lives for Christ and the Congo church.

'This is how we know what love is: Jesus Christ laid down His life for us. And we ought to lay down our lives for our brothers.' *(1 John 3:16)*

The following months brought news of raided and ransacked mission stations. Missionaries were taken and held hostage behind rebel lines; widespread massacre, torture, suspense, doubt and despair. Many known to us were ruthlessly martyred under appalling circumstances. We heard stories of the terrible suffering of the Congolese Christians too, many burnt to death, many buried alive. The Church of Christ in Congo was suffering and rejoicing that they were participating in the sufferings of Christ.

'This reward will be real joy when the glory of the Lord is revealed.' (1 Peter 4:13)

Our hearts ached for Congo and its people.

....oOo....

8 : Our disappointments are God's appointments

Thus we settled down to life in the United Kingdom with our little family and began to pick up the threads of general medical practice in London. We were fortunate to obtain a semi-basement flat in Camden Road, right opposite the surgery but, amidst the constant roar of traffic and the general bustle of day to day activities, we found city life a tremendous contrast to the slow beat of Africa. I was still somewhat constricted in my activities and the children found it particularly hard to adjust to such a different environment; they did not even recognise a bus when they saw one, and they could not understand the necessity to keep away from the busy roads. School was a very new experience for them; even their toys were different.

The medical practice was a large one; there were usually 70-80 patients to see at morning surgery, with a similarly crowded evening surgery as well. Between these busy sessions were some 30 visits around the district, often with emergency interruptions, to say nothing of frequent night calls. The doctor who owned the practice invited James to become a partner with him and as we had now become resigned to the fact that we would not be returning to Africa, he considered the proposal. Our financial resources had sunk to rock bottom and we needed a good source of income to set up home again and settle the children into schools, to say nothing of all the day to day expenses which seemed so enormous after the life we had been used to. Thus, James accepted the offer and was glad to have a secure job, despite its busyness.

After two years, with the aid of a family legacy, we were able to move to a much nicer house in the delightful area of Hampstead and Highgate, near to Kenwood and Hampstead Heath. It was a much better environment for the children and we all enjoyed spreading out once again. As my health improved I found myself able to enjoy a more normal pattern once more, enjoying all the involvement of normal family events. The children started

The family on return from Africa

an 'Animal Hotel' and looked after people's pets while they were away; we had rabbits, guinea pigs, mice, hamsters and budgies, in addition to our growing menagerie of a rabbit, a guinea pig, hamsters, cat and dog, and later a bush baby, for which a special cage was necessary. I learnt to drive and this was a great help as the girls grew up. I became a member of the Zoological Society and being quite near to the London Zoo, we were able to visit there quite often, much to the delight of the children. The excellent library there was a great help when writing a series of articles on animal, insect and bird life in Africa.

There are amusing sides to everything if you look for them, and we certainly had our share within the practice. There was the time when a patient came to the surgery with an ear complaint, for instance. James prescribed some capsules to be taken orally at regular intervals and told the patient to return in a week when the course of antibiotics was finished. Next day she was back again in the crowded surgery.

'Why have you returned?' asked James. 'I told you to come back in a week for me to check the ear.'

'But, doctor, I've got two in there; I can't get any more in,' she replied, 'and I still have the pain!'

I remember one particular night call on a cold, frosty night. The roads were icy and the call was down Holloway Hill; it sounded urgent. James hastened on his way, went into a skid at the top of Holloway Hill and landed up paying respects to a lamp post! He left the damaged car, walked some distance to the house in question, only to be told that the patient was asleep, so there was no need for his assistance! Eventually, incidents like this and very many others, ceased to be amusing as family life was being disrupted and nerves were beginning to fray; the whole thing was becoming a rat race. As James got to know some of the 'regulars' at surgery, so he would start to write out a prescription as they entered the room. After all, he could only allow two minutes a patient when there were always so many patients to be seen.

'I can't go on like this,' he said one day. 'I just can't practise medicine this way; one of these days something serious will be missed and I will be to blame for negligence. I must give my patients more time.'

It was while staying at St. Julian's Community - a Rest Centre at Coolham, Sussex - in the spring of 1962 that the Lord revealed to us how very necessary it was to stop once in a while, to come away and recharge spiritual, physical and mental batteries. It was our first experience of a centre like St. Julian's, where one could do this. There was time to relax, read, rest and walk; time to let our minds unwind and reassess the circumstances that now involved us. At St. Julian's in those days, the children were cared for in a separate house - a walk across the fields - so there were no family responsibilities to disturb our train of thought and contemplation. Even meals were silent, and every evening we met in the little chapel with its straw covered floor, in quiet meditation, experiencing a closeness to God which brought us into His presence with boldness; His peace filling our very beings. Frustrations of past months began to shrink from mountains into molehills; we could think more clearly again and we gained complete confidence that the Lord had control of the future.

Although this centre was basically Anglican, we met others from various denominational backgrounds, all benefiting from what St. Julian's had to offer. So our Baptist ministers, missionaries and friends came particularly to mind as we wondered how possible it would be for us to consider a similar centre of this nature. It seemed that the Lord had created within both of us the ability to be pioneers, and already we had experienced various situations when this gift had made itself relevant. As this new consideration came to our minds, and as we thought and prayed about it, the more we began to realise that the Lord really was speaking to us.

We returned to Hampstead with a new enthusiasm and anticipation as to what the next step would be, and with complete confidence that this new vision was about to emerge into reality.

We were so sure that our paths were leading us on in the direction of creating a Rest Home or Retreat Centre, that we started hunting for a suitable property. We were prepared to search to within a 30-40 mile radius of London - this we felt was the area upon which we should concentrate. One of the first properties that came to our notice was in Haslemere, Surrey; we did not know the district and, although the property sounded good according to the brochure, we cast the information to one side, because it was far too expensive. We saw many properties within the set radius, but none of them seemed to be right. However, we were sure that we were doing the right thing and that, in due course, the right property would be found.

It was at that time that James was approached by the Baptist Missionary Society, with whom we had served in Congo. Would he consider an appointment on the Home Staff of the Society as their Medical Director? Was this God opening further doors of service for which we had been trained? The appointment would involve the medical examinations and health checks for the large number of BMS overseas missionaries, and general overseeing of the medical work of the Society. It would also entail launching a special medical appeal to Churches in the whole Baptist denomination, to raise a large sum of money to upgrade and re-equip the Society's hospitals and medical centres in many lands. A tremendous challenge and opportunity, but we had faced similar challenges before. Could this be linked with a Retreat Centre for Ministers and Missionaries, and was God enlarging our small vision and challenging us to take up an even greater task, to follow in the footsteps of the great pioneer and missionary statesman - the late Sir Clement C. Chesterman - who was then about to retire as Medical Secretary of the B.M.S?

As yet, no suitable property had been found but, as we prayed, it became clear that this was God answering our own prayers and longings to serve Him, and that we must act. We, therefore, took an enormous step of faith, and James resigned from the Health Service and the lucrative practice. It would mean giving up not only a partnership and eventual succession in a few years to a large medical practice, but also a large income and pension scheme, to return to a missionary salary - were we being 'fools for Christ's sake'? (1 Corinthians 4:10)

Soon after this decision came the acceptance by the Committee of the B.M.S. of James for the new post as Medical Director of the Society, the appointment to begin some nine months later.

By the late autumn of 1962, with our resignation from the Health Service taking effect on 31st December, we had progressed no further in our search for a property and we were beginning to get concerned. Surely, if the Lord meant us to open up a Centre for His people, then by now we would have been clearly led to the right property.

We now started to search the Hindhead, Haslemere district, and somehow something clicked. This was the area; we felt quite certain about it. The Lord was obviously settling this point in our minds, having first got us touring just about every other place within a 40-mile radius of London! We were so certain about the area that we sought out the schools and got the girls booked in for the January term without having a clue where we would be living. This was just one of the many occasions when we had to go ahead in faith. It had happened before and it was to happen again.

Never underestimate faith. If you feel certain that you are on the right wavelength in the will of the Lord, and under the power of the Holy Spirit, act. Remember the Red Sea, Abraham and Isaac and so many examples given to us in Scripture, where God's people needed to act in faith before the answer was revealed. We need to be sensible and sensitive in these situations. Spend much time in prayer and often receive advice and counsel from one who can help in a practical and spiritual level, but the Lord does not expect us to sit and wait for something to happen - unless He specifically tells us to 'be still'. (Ps. 46) When something is happening, he expects us to move.

We had found a house at Churt, near Frensham, and set a ceiling price, but the owner refused to negotiate the price. So we felt this was not the Lord's choice for us, but our choice for Him! How patient the Lord is with us when we make mistakes or go ahead under our own stream. When we later thought back to that property, we realised that it would have been totally unsuitable for the development that evolved; we just praised Him for putting a stumbling block in our way!

Suddenly, we remembered one of the first properties that had been sent to us; it was actually within the area to which we had been so definitely guided. We looked out the information, made further enquiries, and discovered that it was still on the market. It had even been up for auction during the summer and had not sold. We knew that it was more expensive than we ever thought we could afford, but nevertheless we felt constrained to go and see it. Have you ever walked into something or come across something and felt it was just the right thing? This is how we felt with Marley Manor. The moment we crossed the threshold it seemed as if the Lord was saying 'This is the place'. If so, He would have to intervene with some finance, for this property had a very high asking price, far beyond our present means!

It seemed that the Lord was really testing us over this, because suddenly two other bidders appeared from nowhere for this delightful property, so the price went even higher, but still we felt we had found the place of God's choosing. One bidder dropped out as the price rose still higher, and we had to make our decision. Our London house had not yet sold and, as yet, we had not got enough finance to lay down a 10% deposit on this one!

As we prayed long into the night, we felt that we were on the brink of tremendous things and now we were quite certain that we must go forward in faith, trusting in the God of the impossible.

Next day we contacted the vendor's Solicitor, who informed us that, as both bidders now remaining in the final attempt to purchase Marley Manor felt they had reached their ceiling offer (ours had been reached before we even started bidding!), it would be sold to the party who first delivered the signed contract to purchase. We were now so sure that the Lord's seal was on this deal that we immediately took one of the biggest steps of faith we had ever taken, signed the contract and rushed it round to the vendor's Solicitor. It arrived just an hour before a larger offer, which could have finally taken Marley Manor out of our reach! But we only had a short period to raise the necessary finance which had to be found almost immediately to complete the purchase, and we had no idea how this could be done! We could only rest on the promise of *Eph. 3:20*.

'Now to Him who is able to do immeasurably more than all we ask or imagine, according to His power that is at work within us...'

....oOo....

9 : Marley Manor and the Medical Appeal

Conscious of the fact that we had to act without delay, it was necessary to place our London home immediately into the Auctioneer's hands. We realised that the house and grounds would have to sell at more than double the purchase price to get anywhere near the price of Marley Manor. In addition, many more thousands of pounds would be needed to furnish and equip the new Centre.

There were two properties in the same area up for auction; the first did not sell and was withdrawn. There were very few people at the auction and there were moments when our spirits felt very low. But, prior to the auction, words from Scripture had encouraged us and we tried not to let our natural nervous and anxious tendencies take over.

Marley Manor Guest and Conference Centre, Haslemere, Surrey

'Have not I commanded you? Be strong and courageous. Do not be terrified; do not be discouraged, for the Lord your God will be with you...' (Joshua 1:9)

Bidding started and the price rose rapidly, until it became obvious that only two bidders were seriously attempting to outbid each other. Our prayer was 'Lord, keep them at it!' - the only time we had seriously prayed for two people to fight it out! - Still the bidding went up, gradually slowing down until it was fought out in £50 bids, and faltered just £50 short of the tremendous reserve price we had felt led to place on it. We gave the OK and the deal was clinched. The Lord had enabled the seemingly impossible to happen and now we knew He had provided all we needed to go forward. Once more we had committed ourselves to a work which would need a tremendous step in faith to fulfil. We were very conscious of our need of the Lord's guidance and wisdom through the power of the Holy Spirit every step of the way.

Moving day was to be January 12th 1963. On Boxing Day that Christmas, it snowed heavily, and the winter progressed with abnormal falls of snow. By January there was no sign of a let-up. Pipes froze and burst and everywhere it was bitterly cold. It was doubtful whether the move would be possible, because reports from the previous owner of Marley Manor indicated that snow was exceptionally deep and the lane up to the Manor almost impassable, certainly for heavy traffic like removal vans. However, the day arrived and the removal vans came as planned. We warned the firm of conditions and suggested that the men brought some snow gear and also some food, as we would be some way from the shops! They provided neither!

Marley Lane took some negotiating, but we finally made it and awaited the removal vans. It was mid-day before the first van arrived but, on negotiating the turn into the drive, it went into a deep snow drift and no amount of manoeuvring would dislodge it. Finally, we had to get a local building firm to come and remove a gate post and, eventually, the vans arrived at the front door at about 3.00 p.m. It was dark long before the unloading was complete, and everything was just piled into the house to be distributed the next day. The men decided it was too late to finish the job that day, so we put two up for the night and used what little food we had to share between us.

Outside, conditions were no better the next day, and we had to get the children to their new school and go for some provisions. Impacted, icy snow on the roads did not make this an easy task, but we were not dismayed, and soon the chaos of furniture, etc., was well on the way to being sorted out and the men departed. Now we were faced with the task of planning and preparing this house for its future service, and a real challenge presented itself to us. God had provided; now our task had really begun.

James had decided to take a few months' sabbatical, to get the preliminaries of settling in as near complete as possible before accepting the post at the Baptist Missionary Society. Every moment of this time was necessary.

Soon after we took up residence at Marley Manor, Miss Kathleen Hasler came to stay for a couple of weeks, whilst recovering from influenza. Kathleen was the hostess at the Baptist Missionary Society headquarters and had done so much in the planning and equipping of missionary furlough homes. She was a very dear friend of ours and was one of the first people to share our thoughts and plans about the idea of a Christian centre. Kathleen had followed with interest the progress of the project and had given advice and help all along the way. Whilst with us, she helped us to plan and list necessary equipment for the centre and was with us again later, when the various items arrived. It was really great to have her around, and we talked of the time when she might be able to join us in the work here, following retirement from the Baptist Missionary Society.

However, this was not to be. The last time she stayed with us in the March of 1963, she complained of some internal trouble. It was necessary for this to be investigated in London and an operation revealed advanced malignancy. She only lived until May, when the Lord called her home. We cannot begin to tell you how lost we felt. With all her experience and help we had felt we could go forward with confidence but now we were to go forward alone, trusting completely in the Lord for the task He had given us to do.

But His promises, as always, encouraged us to press on and go ahead with the development of Marley Manor as a Christian centre. We had been able to purchase, with the house, curtains and carpets, lighting fixtures and a fully equipped kitchen so, after a visit to the January furniture sales, we were able to start taking guests in a fully furnished house in March, just a few weeks after our arrival. The house was officially opened and dedicated to the glory of God by Sir Cyril Black, M.P., on June 22nd, 1963, and a big crowd attended this first official public function.

At this stage we felt the Lord wanted us to prepare to serve individual guests, particularly those in full-time Christian ministry. We would endeavour to provide an atmosphere of peace and tranquillity, where people could come and unwind. Breakfast in bed, the day free to rest, to walk or sit in the garden, closing the day with the Lord in evening devotions.

Kathleen had spoken of the need for a little chapel on the hillside. We had even been there together to discuss the site. She had been so anxious that this should be a place where people could come and find peace and spiritual refreshment. It seemed fitting, therefore, that we should erect a little Chapel in her memory, and we made this known to her many contacts and friends. Donations came in from far and wide, and we felt this was a seal from the Lord that this was the first step of development upon which we should embark.

The Chapel project was, therefore, launched in the autumn and winter of 1963, and on July 18th, 1964, we had the joy of dedicating this little building on the hillside to the service of God in this centre. We had arranged a large plate glass picture window, looking out over the Weald of Sussex, to be situated behind the Communion table, and this never failed to convey a sense of God's presence to the visitor. Above the window we chose a favourite text of Kathleen's, 'Be still and know that I am God'. *(Ps. 46:10 A.V.)*

How many people shared in the building and furnishing of the Chapel! The builder of the Chapel was from the United Reformed Church. The curtains and carpets were made by a member of the Brethren Assembly, chairs and table were supplied by the Methodist Church, the text was written by a Catholic sign writer. The organ was given by Kathleen's family and kneelers were made by a variety of people, and prayer books provided by a local Anglican church. The Chapel was dedicated and opened by the Rev. George Sterry, who was then Minister of the Baptist Church, Hampstead, which was Kathleen's church and the church we had attended whilst living in Hampstead. Some 250 guests came to this second public gathering and memorial occasion and, on the day of the opening of the Chapel, we rejoiced that the building and its contents were fully paid for and the builder's bill met in full. Once more we had seen the good hand of the Lord upon us.

And so the work of Marley Manor developed, as a steady stream of guests from all walks of life visited us. Gradually we saw the purpose of Marley Manor being fulfilled as men and women were revitalised and returned to their spheres of life and service with fresh heart and a new vision after times spent at the centre.

James took up his post as Medical Director of the Baptist Missionary Society in 1963 and travelled up daily to their headquarters at Baker Street. This made a heavy workload for me, supervising the centre, running the children to and from school, shopping and other duties, to say nothing of the garden and grounds, extending to twelve acres! I was so grateful that the Lord had healed me sufficiently to be able to cope with such a full programme and very little help. But so often before we had proved His overall undertaking in seemingly impossible situations.

Apart from James' routine medical work for the Society, his first big task was to organise a special medical appeal. With his knowledge of the conditions in medical missionary hospitals, and our own experiences in Africa, he felt well equipped for the job, and accepted the challenge with enthusiasm. The Society had been challenged about the state of disrepair, shortage of equipment and lack of drugs. How well we had known these situations! The needs were tremendous and the committees unanimously agreed that something must be done about the situation of the Society.

So in May 1964, at the annual missionary rally of the Baptist Assembly meetings, a special medical appeal was launched under James' leadership. The appeal was to run for two years and the target was to be £100,000. This was the minimum amount agreed to be necessary to upgrade, rebuild, repair and re-equip hospitals and dispensaries of the Baptist Missionary Society overseas. This meant a heavy deputation programme, visiting a large number of Baptist churches throughout the British Isles.

A large thermometer chart was displayed in the entrance hall of the Baptist Missionary Society headquarters, and over the coming months this gradually rose. All kinds of projects and schemes were initiated as a means of raising the funds in all the Baptist churches round the country. Everyone interested in the medical crisis overseas pulled their weight in one way or another. The Sunday School collecting scheme alone raised several thousand pounds. An audio-visual presentation was produced which, in a series of colour transparencies, showed the contrast between European standards of medicine and conditions pertaining to medical work overseas. This contrast so stirred the Society's supporters that the fund really started to roll and the thermometer chart began to gather momentum.

During this extensive deputation programme, various gifts were donated in the form of specific medical items. Some of these items were high-quality equipment, which was being made available through changing techniques in this country and was, therefore, surplus to needs. This was exciting and, in many cases, arrangements were made to ship out pieces of equipment direct to a destination overseas. Most of the equipment donated was probably a year or two behind the latest modern scientific equipment being used in this country, but was something like twenty-five years ahead of much of the equipment being used in hospitals overseas. To give one example, the London Clinic donated a superb x-ray unit: how often we had longed for one like that!

These donations of gifts in kind began to snowball as we met more medical personnel during the deputation programme. Our concern, however, was how to ship out this specialised equipment without drawing from the actual medical appeal fund. Packing cost money and so did shipping, but these opportunities were too good to miss. We need not have been concerned; the Lord again had everything under control, and a Christian Shipping Company suddenly sprang up from nowhere and offered to get the equipment shipped out free of charge. Bills used to arrive at the B.M.S. medical office stamped 'PAID'. This was a tremendously generous gesture on behalf of the Company, and we praised the Lord that He never does things by halves.

But these gift items of equipment gave rise to further investigation. It appeared that there was an enormous reservoir of equipment available which could be purchased for a fraction of the price that missions were normally having to pay to supply their medical work. The problem at this stage was, where could this equipment be stored? It ranged from hospital furniture to instruments and equipment of every kind. This surplus and redundant equipment was being sold to scrap merchants all over the country, and then being re-sold at considerable profit.

One day, James was called to a hospital in London to see an x-ray unit that had been offered to a missionary society, which he had been asked to see on their behalf. This London hospital was re-building on a new site and had a lot more equipment available, but the Baptist Missionary Society had no facilities to cope with such a consignment. A few days later, a phone call came through the medical department of the B.M.S. A scrap merchant was on the line.

'Morning, guv,' called a Cockney voice. 'I've got some nice 'orspital beds I was told you might be interested in. Only £5 each.'

On turning down the offer, further investigations were made and it was discovered that these beds, together with hundreds of pounds' worth of other equipment, had been bought by the scrap merchant from the London hospital that was being re-sited, for a total of £10 to clear the building; he was going to make a tremendous profit!

So the medical appeal was completed at the beginning of 1966. What a triumph; the thermometer chart had soared to the top and overshot the target to settle at £107,000. On top of this, many thousands of pounds' worth of good quality medical equipment had been donated and shipped to destinations overseas at no cost to the Society.

The day finally arrived as, in the crowded Westminster Chapel at the Baptist Union Spring Assembly of that year, the total was announced. Quite spontaneously, the great congregation present rose to sing the Doxology, praise to the Lord who made it all possible, and thanks to so many who had participated in one way or another.

....oOo....

10 : A vision realised

The triumphant Assembly meeting at Westminster was by no means the end. While James was involved in his travels to raise the £100,000 target to upgrade the medical work of the Baptist Missionary Society, he began to notice how much medical equipment was surplus to requirements in our British hospitals through their re-building programmes. He could not get the picture of the medical contrasts at home and overseas out of his mind. He realised, too, that it was not just the Baptist Mission hospitals and dispensaries that were desperate for help, but medical mission work of every denomination the world over. We shared a common problem: shortage of medical equipment and spiralling costs. Having worked in such conditions ourselves, with desperate shortages, we were in a position to realise how much our colleagues, struggling to maintain a high standard of medical work with a minimum of equipment, would appreciate this surplus stock. Now, the seed sown and conceived in the heart of Africa began to emerge as a vision.

Our minds began to toss the situation; rather than let this surplus equipment be thrown out to scrap merchants, couldn't a united organisation be set up to serve all societies with medical work overseas? This would seem to be a good way of utilising the enormous reservoir of equipment apparently available from National Health Service hospitals in the United Kingdom. Such an organisation could purchase and then supply all Christian mission hospitals throughout the world with the tools and equipment necessary for their work.

We considered this prayerfully over a period of time. Everyone we spoke to seemed to be enthusiastic, but more than enthusiasm was needed; we had to make quite sure that this whole vision was of the Lord. It was very tempting to consider staying with the Baptist Missionary Society and to have the joy of helping to spend the money we had raised through the appeal, but what of all those other hospitals of all denominations of the Christian church which also needed re-equipping and supplying? Couldn't a Medical Missionary Ministry of Supply be created to ease this growing world-wide problem?

After much prayerful consideration and clear guidance, James felt certain that he should pursue the vision he had; the burden of the desperate need for medical help, both to assist the workers and to relieve the sufferers was so great. A verse of Scripture came to us as we considered the situation and the opportunities.

'Inasmuch as ye have done it unto one of the least of these my brethren ye have done it unto me.' (Matt. 25:40)

For the first time, we began to realise why God had taken us through missionary and Bible School training and sent us to Africa. For the first time we realised that, without the experience we had gained, building up and working in a mission hospital in the middle of Africa, struggling to develop a medical work under very primitive conditions, we could not have appreciated the very real medical needs overseas, as we saw them now. It all began to make sense; God had been training us over the years for this very task. So started another chapter in our experiences.

James decided to approach the Medical Committee of the Conference of British Missionary Societies (C.B.M.S.) to put forward his vision. They were most enthusiastic and suggested that, if he got such an organisation going, they would be prepared to back him. The outcome was a massive research operation into the viability of such a scheme, and reactions gathered from medical mission centres overseas, through their societies, as to the need and desire for such a service. There was an immediate, positive response, so now, more definite plans could be made.

The Medical Committee of the C.B.M.S. appointed Colonel Bovan of the Salvation Army to become Administrative Secretary, and James to become Medical Director to the new organisation. Thus, in 1966, the Joint Mission Hospital Equipment Board (J.M.H.E.B.) was launched, designed to run for a period of two years, this amount of time being considered adequate, to use up the surplus hospital equipment then available in the U.K.

During the summer, James left the B.M.S. to devote more time to the creation of the J.M.H.E.B. and to spend time with Colonel Bovan, to discuss possible staffing and other matters. Also, they prepared a memorandum for Mission Boards. This was designed to help the missions with their initial notifications to their medical centres overseas, concerning the new scheme. Costs to societies would be nominal for the purchase of equipment, packing, insurance and shipping, plus a small service charge.

It was necessary to find a centre from which the organisation could operate. The late Colonel Anderson (Medical Officer of the Salvation Army) was a great friend and advisor during those early days, and he made some enquiries about the possibilities of using the Men's Social Service Centre of the Salvation Army in Bermondsey, London, which would provide 2,500 sq. feet of temporary storage and office accommodation. The Salvation Army readily agreed to rent the premises to the J.M.H.E.B. for a nominal rent of £400 a year and kindly took on the job of making the building suitable for the new organisation. This building had once been an old stable; it needed to be weatherproofed and the floor levelled for a start. Then they partitioned off two offices, decorated throughout and installed gas-fired central heating, thus transforming the building into a small modern warehouse and office complex.

It was at this point that James, Colonel Anderson and Colonel Bovan went to visit the Ministry of Health to ask if they could help in any way to transfer good quality medical supplies, surplus to requirements in the United Kingdom hospitals, to the under-developed countries of the world. The Ministry were delighted at the idea of a joint organisation being formed to make use of the redundant equipment which was continually being produced. To date there had never been an organisation operating along these lines, so they wholeheartedly agreed to back up the enterprise, and notify every hospital in the United Kingdom of the formation of the J.M.H.E.B., and the 'bona fide' nature of the organisation to receive medical equipment surplus to hospital requirements. Links were also made with the Ministry of Overseas Development to establish correct relationships.

While the building at Bermondsey was being prepared, the initial work of the J.M.H.E.B. operated from Marley Manor. James employed a local secretary, Mrs Mary Arlidge (later to work at Bermondsey with her husband) and also had some other part-time secretarial help. Together they began to answer the mass of correspondence from home and overseas. James also spent a considerable amount of time building up a panel of advisors around the country in order to make contact with the Regional Hospital Boards. Mrs. Winn, one of the part-time secretaries, operated from the Headquarters of the C.B.M.S., her main job being to list requests from overseas. A questionnaire had been sent to hundreds of hospitals overseas, asking for their reactions and some idea of their equipment needs. We were staggered at the response. Soon lists were compiled of 100,000 requests for medical instruments and equipment; we stopped counting at 200,000 requests!

At this stage, the C.B.M.S. wrote round to member missions to ask for the necessary financial support to launch the organisation. £3,500 a year for two years was promised by twenty-one sponsoring missions.

Additional finance of a further £3,500 was provided by Oxfam and Christian Aid. This created a working budget of £7,000 per annum. It was not considered right to receive grants for any longer than was necessary as the organisation did not want to deflect money given for missionary work into the J.M.H.E.B. By the volume of goods sent overseas, we wanted to be able to create an organisation that needed no support from the Societies we were asked to serve.

James started officially with the J.M.H.E.B. on September 1st, 1966, in a part-time capacity, as he still needed to spend a certain amount of time assisting with the running and developing of Marley Manor, as well as continuing to examine medically patients for missions and Christian organisations.

The C.B.M.S. now advised the setting up of a Council of Management to consist of twelve members, and during the summer, James and Colonel Bovan had been in contact with a number of prominent people who enthusiastically agreed to serve. Lord Porritt, who was then Sir Arthur Porritt - surgeon to the Queen - graciously agreed to back the new organisation and become its first Chairman. When, at the end of 1967, Sir Arthur Porritt went to New Zealand as Governor General, he agreed to become President, and Sir John Richardson - Senior Consultant Physician of St. Thomas's Hospital - became Chairman; in later years, Lord Richardson took over from Lord Porritt as our President.

Eleven other members of the Council of Management were drawn from Missionary Societies and Christian representatives in Industry, Shipping and Hospital Supplies. The first Council Meeting was in November, 1966. It was tragic that Mr. Hawkins of A. L. Hawkins & Co. died whilst on his way to the meeting. This firm had helped to supply medical equipment to mission hospitals for many years, and Mr. Hawkins had been a keen and enthusiastic advocate of the principle of a joint mission hospital equipment service.

By October, 1966, we were all set to go. The building at Bermondsey was now ready for occupation and our first real headquarters could begin to operate. Colonel Bovan moved in and Mrs. Winn became his secretary. They both worked full-time and formed the first real nucleus of the operation. As the work of the organisation developed, further staff were employed. With the increasing volume of goods being handled for export, Mr. Tony West, a state registered nurse who had worked as hospital manager with the Leprosy Mission in Korea, joined our staff. At the December Committee Meeting, 1966, it was agreed to employ a full-time stores assistant and to purchase a small van, capable of collecting non-bulky articles. A stacking truck for the warehouse would also be necessary.

Now we began an extensive itinerary programme throughout the United Kingdom, to make known the existence of J.M.H.E.B. and what it was trying to do. We visited all Regional Hospital Boards in England, Scotland, Wales and Ireland. Most of these trips were done by road, but when we visited Scotland, we started from London airport at 8.00 a.m. one morning and reached Glasgow an hour later for a morning appointment. Next day we drove on to Dundee for a morning appointment and to Aberdeen in the afternoon. Next morning we left the car at the airport and flew through a blizzard over snow-capped mountains by a small plane to Inverness for a morning appointment. We hired a car for the day, completed our visits, returned to the airport in the evening, left the car and flew back to London. We had covered 1,500 miles in sixty hours!

At the outset, much of our equipment was obtained as surplus to British hospital requirements, due to changing techniques and hospital re-building programmes. We usually travelled to see the stocks available at a particular hospital; this involved many thousands of miles during the first year. Sometimes the equipment offered was not suitable or practical and had to be refused; it would not have been worth paying transport to collect it to clutter up the already rapidly filling warehouse. On the other hand, anything that was of reasonable scrap value we included in selected consignments, because this could then be carefully stripped down to be sold as scrap - steel, copper, brass, etc. The price received for this scrap provided precious additional funds for the small but growing organisation.

All second-hand equipment was renovated to render it, if possible, 'as good as new'. We had no proper facilities during the first year and space was limited, so most equipment at this stage had to be renovated and refurbished by outside firms.

Supplies began rolling in from all over the place. Stainless steel ware was going out in the hospitals of this country, because of the introduction of synthetic polypropylene and other ware. Thousands of stainless steel articles, therefore, became available to the organisation, many of them unused, straight off the stock shelves of hospital stores. For instance, on one occasion we purchased 600 new wash bowls for £30; these were valued at £5 each. It was at this point that two incredible miracles took place, proving that we were indeed serving the 'God of the impossible'.

The phone rang. 'Have you heard about ....? Their entire stock of new medical equipment of all types is to be sold in a bankruptcy sale, valued at £100,000. Are you interested?' The caller was an official at the Ministry of Health and he had called us to notify us about a well known medical equipment firm who had run into financial difficulties and had become bankrupt.

James answered. 'We would be very interested.'

'If you are prepared to offer any sum in excess of £40,000, you would stand a good chance of obtaining some of the stock, I think,' replied the caller.

'That's impossible,' thought James. 'We only have £600 in the bank, but I'm not going to let an opportunity like this pass by unnoticed; I'll go and have a look and see what's going. I might get some items.' So, James went along to 'view' and was soon gasping at what he saw. Here was a large, modern warehouse packed to the ceiling with brand new medical equipment and how he coveted it all for the mission hospitals of the world!

He put in a bid of the entire J.M.H.E.B. reserve, £600, hoping to get some items at least. We were bitterly disappointed when the offer was turned down in favour of a commercial scrap merchant, who had offered £1,500 to clear the building. If only we had even £1,600 to offer a higher bid! But we had prayed about this and God knew the desperate needs of those for whom we wanted this equipment overseas, and we were trusting Him for our supplies.

Two weeks later, the Solicitors involved in the sale rang. 'Good morning, Sir,' called a cheery gentleman. 'I've just rung to tell you that the commercial scrap firm concerned with the bankruptcy sale has been unable to raise their £1,500, and we are wondering if you are still interested.'

'Of course, we're still interested,' retorted James, hardly able to prevent his excitement breaking into a loud 'Hallelujah!'

'But, you would have to be prepared to clear the building of EVERYTHING; then your offer of £600 will be accepted. Is that possible?' asked the calm, cheery gentleman.

'Leave it to us, and thank you.' James slammed down the receiver and almost leapt over his desk to break the news to Colonel Bovan. Their joy exploded into peals of laughter as they considered the sheer impossibility of purchasing thousands of items of new medical equipment for just £600. Surely God was setting the seal with a solid foundation of stock with which to set J.M.H.E.B. on the move. Praise rang through our 'stable' headquarters to dominate all other activities that day!

Colonel Bovan and James remembered the verse in *Malachi 3:10.*

'Bring ye all the tithes into the storehouse and prove me now herewith, saith the Lord of Hosts, if I will not open to you the windows of heaven and pour you out such a blessing that you will not be able to contain it.'

We were surely experiencing the reality of this verse but God had not finished surprising us yet. We hadn't recovered from this miracle before an even greater one occurred. The next surprise phone call came from the Ministry of Defence.

'We're disposing of some medical equipment,' said the man at the other end, 'and we have been informed that you might like to inspect it for possible use in your organisation.'

'Thank you,' said James. 'We would be interested to see it,' and he expounded a bit more about J.M.H.E.B. to the interested caller, who then explained that this equipment had been stored against a possible atomic emergency.

So, with directions and instructions, James went to inspect the said equipment. To his utter amazement, he was taken to a vast five square mile underground vault, and there before him were enough medical stores to fill a host of hospitals; it was one vast Aladdin's Cave.

'Put down anything you're interested in,' said the accompanying guide, and handed James a block board.

That was an unwise move on the part of the guide! James wrote as fast as his pen would travel, utterly speechless and agog with amazement; this must be a dream. Did this guide mistake him for a commercial buyer for some vast international consortium? For a start, there were 500,00 new surgical instruments of every type, and a vast amount of every kind of hospital equipment and furniture. James just kept on writing on his block board!

'Thank you,' said James at the end of the tour, in a most calm and dignified manner (so opposite to his internal feelings!). 'I will get my secretary to type out an official list of all the items we would like to purchase and submit our offer to the Ministry of Defence.'

As he left the vault his head was reeling as he considered how half a million surgical instruments, plus millions of pounds' worth of brand new equipment could be used to re-equip mission hospitals throughout the world. 'Well, it could only be a dream,' he thought. 'Where would that sort of money come from anyhow?' But God was in all this, and that was where the difference between impossible and possible lay.

James put in an offer of £1,000 (all that J.M.H.E.B. possessed at the time) and, 'sticking his neck out' he asked for all he had seen.

'Surely, nothing could be gained by such a ridiculous offer,' he thought, but he was to be proved wrong.

A few days later a letter arrived from the Ministry of Defence. 'In view of the valuable nature of your organisation's work,' it read, 'and the fact that all you requested will be used to help the poorer nations overseas, we accept your offer.'

James took off round the half-packed shelves of disposable syringes, waving the precious paper wildly in the air.

'He's done it again, Colonel,' he yelled. 'God has made the impossible possible again; look at this,' and together they once more praised the Lord and excitedly toured 'the stable' to see wherever all this vast hoard could be stacked.

Thus, a few days later, a fleet of lorries arrived with 17.5 tons of new medical equipment and half a million new surgical instruments. God was certainly adding to the solid foundation of stock needed to set us on the move.

These two miracles were surely the start of the fantastic story of a fantastic organisation, designed to transform medical mission and relief work worldwide. From this point we never turned back.

Supplies were also obtained from manufacturers who donated stocks surplus to requirements. For example, we had several gifts of £1,000 worth of new surgical instruments, and one day an enormous pantechnicon rolled up, loaded with one and a half tons of disposable syringes as a gift. On another occasion we were able to obtain some old hospital beds for $12^{1}/_{2}$p each. After refurbishing, they were as good as new. As time went on, we were able to supply everything from minor equipment to hospital furniture, x-ray equipment, operating tables, electro-diagnostic equipment, etc. All was examined, sorted, recorded and cleaned.

By the beginning of 1968, 65 consignments had been despatched, including 400 beds and cots and two x-ray units, 40 operating tables, three autoclaves, six obstetric beds, 1,200 miscellaneous instruments, quantities of suture material, sterilizers, 100 items of ward furniture, two theatre lights and 350 items of stainless steel ware. But still the present demands for items for equipment stood at 200,000. The pressure of work waiting for attention was tremendous!

Our early vision had now become a reality.

....oOo....

11 : Off the launching pad

So J.M.H.E.B. forged ahead to meet the demands of overseas hospitals, and the C.B.M.S. favoured the continuance of this project beyond the initial two years, at first considered adequate. This was because of the obvious demand by medical mission work. J.M.H.E.B. had proved to be practical and a real benefit to mission hospitals abroad. Good working relationships had been established with many Regional Hospital Boards and with the Ministry of Health. A considerable volume of useful material had been secured and despatched to mission hospitals, and savings in cost to missions was considerable.

It was originally thought that the surplus equipment from British hospitals would only be available for a limited time, but experience showed that, because of the modernising of hospitals and of medical advance, the supply of surplus equipment could continue more or less indefinitely.

It was the judgement of the Medical Committee that the savings on costs to hospitals abroad were so considerable that, given a reasonable volume of supplies, the charge to hospitals abroad would be sufficient to cover the administrative costs of J.M.H.E.B. and still represent a considerable saving to missions.

Slowly the volume of consignments sent overseas began to grow; about 250 shipments went out during the first two years, and we received shipping rebates from many of the shipping companies. We used commercial packers for the big consignments during the early days; smaller things we just packed in cartons, which we sent away to be packed.

One day, a big request came in from the Ivory Coast of West Africa, urgently requesting a major x-ray unit. These major x-ray units cost anything from £8,000 to £12,000 at that time. While we were thinking how we could cope with such a request, an offer came to us from a hospital switching over to a new type of modern x-ray equipment. They didn't know what to do with their present model, because no other hospital in the area was wanting that particular type. It was in perfect condition and had been installed for over £8,000 just a couple of years before. They had received one offer from a scrap merchant for £50. We offered them £60!

So this major unit was dismantled by the manufacturers, professionally packed and shipped out to the hospital on the Ivory Coast of West Africa for a total cost of £600. It was soon operational and giving excellent service.

Goods awaiting shipment oversea

We were now not only serving the member societies of the organisation but many other societies with medical work overseas. Although J.M.H.E.B. was set up from the Protestant Conference of British Missionary Societies, it became obvious that its services should be equally shared with the many Catholic mission hospitals round the world. We also began to serve the big charitable bodies - Oxfam, Save the Children Fund, Christian Aid, War on Want, Tear Fund, etc., who came to us for practical help in their outreach to the needs of the world.

In 1969, James and I visited the United States where we were able to link up with the Medical Aid Programme, organised through the Christian Medical Association of America and the Inter-Church Medical Assistance Programme of America. Both these organisations dealt only with drugs. Because of the situation in America, particularly with regard to the federal tax position, American pharmaceutical companies were able to give away millions of dollars' worth of drugs to these two societies. These were passed on for a small documentation and handling charge to mission hospitals throughout the world. We saw the set-up, but at that time we never realised that our organisation would be called to tackle the same problem when these conditions were changed in America.

We also visited the warehouse of the Inter-Church Medical Programme in New England. Liaison was built up with these organisations; they co-operated with us in advertising our goods, which led to many orders of medical equipment for American mission hospitals coming to J.M.H.E.B., thus continuing to develop the ever-widening circle of our work.

We made contact with European Missionary Societies and Christian Agencies and started to supply mission hospitals of different nationalities. In all these ways, the scope of J.M.H.E.B. steadily widened as the Lord opened doors through organisations in many countries. Our goods even reached behind the Iron Curtain to needy Christian causes.

Now, slowly, the organisation was realising its early vision of an international medical missionary 'Ministry of Supply', but storage was becoming a problem. The Salvation Army Centre at Bermondsey let us have another room, but this was still not adequate, and after two years we had to start using storage space at shippers' warehouses to cope with the continuing flow of incoming consignments. This was not ideal and we began to realise that the time had come for us to widen our horizons.

It was at the beginning of 1970 that it became apparent that the facilities at Bermondsey were no longer adequate to cope with the expanding role of

J.M.H.E.B.; also the overcrowded conditions were causing James some concern for the health of the staff. He emphasised to the Committee the urgent need to secure larger premises.

Thus began many months of searching by James and Colonel Bovan to find suitable premises. They inspected many commercial buildings within the London area but none of the available properties seemed to meet the necessary requirements. Then out of the blue one day came particulars concerning a small warehouse in Sutton, Surrey, currently being used by a diamond tool firm. They went to see the premises and, right from the first, these seemed to be just what they had been looking for. The building had started off as 'Alf Govers' Indoor Cricket School' in the 1920's, but now consisted of several offices and a two-storey warehouse, accommodating some forty diamond tool machines.

They soon realised the potential of such a building; it was just a question of finding the £42,000 needed for the freehold! The Council of Management realised the necessity for this step, however, with the organisation growing at such a pace. Adequate funds were just not available for such a development, but it was considered advisable to share this challenge with all the sponsoring missions of the organisation, together with appropriate Trusts. After all, as far as the missions were concerned, they would benefit in the long run by more efficient service from J.M.H.E.B., if it could only take advantage of the obvious need to expand. It would certainly be to their advantage if they could give some financial help at this stage of the organisation's development.

The response from these missions was overwhelming and there was no doubt about their enthusiasm for J.M.H.E.B. continuing to function. Enough finance was assured to complete the purchase of the building by the autumn of 1970.

The next move was to make the building operational. There was a great deal of decorating, alteration and improvement to be done to adapt the premises for our requirements. There was very little finance to spare, so 'Operation Paint Brush' was called into being. There were several sources we could contact for voluntary help; indeed, help was offered to us before we got around to asking for it. Willing Christian nurses from a London teaching hospital spared an hour or so after a busy day on duty; students appeared to lend a hand, and other young people popped in and out for the odd hour or two here and there. The Navigator Organisation, operating in the area, gathered groups at weekends and, in the space of two or three weeks, the dingy premises took on a new appearance as walls and ceilings were painted and the whole interior cleaned up. Some of the more skilled jobs, such as electrical work and floor laying, had to be done by professionals, but with all the voluntary help we were able to keep costs down to a minimum.

Eventually the building of 3,810 square feet of ground floor space and 2,295 square feet of balcony space, together with offices, was completed and we were able to move the contents of the Bermondsey warehouse. The move was made gradually over a period of several months, and the staff was split between the two centres. The old warehouse was finally vacated in June, 1971. Mr E. J. Britt of Baker Britt and Company (Shipping) very kindly donated a Ford 7 cwt van, which was a tremendous help in transporting the smaller equipment, together with our own larger van. Stock was arriving almost daily now, from somewhere around the country, and it was a mammoth task sorting out the new warehouse and getting it operational. We were now able to issue printed lists of stock available, which were sent round to the various missionary societies. There must have been something like £50,000 worth of equipment and instruments in stock at this stage, and hospitals from every quarter of the British Isles were still offering redundant equipment. Some twenty-three hospitals were visited in four months and stocks available to us from the Ministry of Defence and the Department of Home and Health in Scotland were inspected. We were able, for example, to bulk purchase a stock of unused surgical diathermy units from ex-governmental surplus sources and then release them cheaply enough to bring the benefits of these advanced operating techniques within the scope of overseas mission hospitals.

It was necessary to display stock conveniently for medical missionary visitors to select or order the items they needed. To simplify this, all the instruments and small items were arranged in 1,000 display boxes, so that customers could wander round the warehouse with a basket and, as in a supermarket, select the items they required.

Due to J.M.H.E.B.'s expanding role around the world, it was decided to shorten the title of the organisation to ECHO (The Supply of Equipment for Charity Hospitals Overseas) and it is by this title that the organisation began to be known.

So 1971 saw the whole operation becoming much more efficient and streamlined and, in order to cope with the constant flow of intake and output, we had to employ additional staff in all departments. Colonel Bovan, who had so ably directed the administration of J.M.H.E.B. since 1966, retired in September and it was necessary to find the right replacement to head up the administrative side of the work and to move forward to the next stage of development. In every major decision since the conception of ECHO, we had seen the hand of God at work; and this occasion was no exception. Just the right man was available for the job - Mr. William Davies - who had served for the previous twenty-two years in the British Navy in Administration, and who brought his administrative talents and experience into the now rapidly developing ECHO. Colonel Bovan was greatly missed and will always be remembered by those connected with the organisation in the early days; but we could not have hoped for a more able successor.

At this point it was suggested that contact be made and possible support sought from sources outside Great Britain and so, towards the end of 1972, visits were made to the West German Institute of Medical Missions and other organisations, all of whom were most helpful and co-operative.

Lord Porritt returned from New Zealand in 1972, and we were delighted when he agreed to remain President of ECHO. He also accepted an invitation to conduct the official opening of the Headquarters in March 1973.

About 200 people congregated in the Parish Church of St. Nicholas, Sutton, on this occasion, where the Reverend Orchard, the General Secretary of the Conference of British Missionary Societies, conducted a service of dedication. Lord Porritt gave a speech of welcome and traced the history of ECHO, under the able Chairmanship of Sir John Richardson. James spoke about the advance and development of the organisation and outlined some of the future plans. After the service, the Deputy Mayor of Sutton and Cheam and the local Member of Parliament unveiled the name board over the main entrance and then guests were invited to enter the building. Donations following the appeal from the Open Day amounted to £31,024.

It had been suggested by the C.B.M.S. that, as ECHO was growing so rapidly, we ought to seek autonomous charitable status to become an independent missionary charity. In order to achieve this, we had to become a private limited company by guarantee. To comply with the Companies' Act, those societies and charities who had sponsored the early development of the organisation were invited to register as members, thus enjoying closer links in the future development of the organisation.

ECHO represented the first organised and united attempt in the United Kingdom to deal with the acquisition, servicing and transport of equipment to mission hospitals and medical relief work overseas. It could supply very large stocks of medical and surgical equipment to meet crisis calls from the major United Kingdom Charities and other Christian bodies for the disaster areas of the world. It was now supporting many hundreds of doctors and nurses working in primitive conditions in the under-developed world, making a unique contribution to the reduction of world suffering. By 1973 nearly 2,000 shipments, postal packages and air freighted consignments had been sent to 611 hospitals in 65 countries. One consignment weighed thirty tons. Hospitals of all Protestant and Catholic denominations and nationalities were served. Charitable missions from many other countries in the Western World were now seeking help from the organisation, so that some ten per cent of the material was, in fact, being distributed through non-British Agencies, Oxfam, Christian Aid, Save the Children Fund, War on Want, Tear Fund and the Catholic Fund for Overseas Development: all came for practical help.

Thoracic surgical equipment and other supplies for Peruvian earthquake victims were requested, supplied and delivered to the Peruvian Embassy in London within 24 hours of the initial request. We also supplied medical needs for the appalling conditions in Bangladesh and for the Ethiopian cholera epidemic, as well as other disaster calls. One day there was a telephone call from Bethlehem. Their x-ray had broken down and needed a new tube. We contacted the manufacturers and arranged to air-freight the necessary part without delay.

The Sutton warehouse soon became stocked to the roof with medical supplies and every available space was taken up. Half a million instruments were in stock, for use in every surgical and medical situation. Hospital

Second home at Sutton

equipment arrived almost daily: wheelchairs, sterilizers, incubators, intensive care units, anaesthetic equipment, x-ray units, hospital furniture, lights and laboratory equipment. All were carefully checked to ensure a perfect product and, where necessary, reconditioning and refurbishing was undertaken. Now, most of the respraying and refurbishing of second-hand equipment was done on the premises, as well as renovating and minor repairs.

There was progress in other directions too. The 'Kalamazoo' business system was introduced and this streamlined the whole system of order processing and control and the maintenance of an up-to-date catalogue stock. Also we now had a 35 cwt. van and a 7 cwt. Ford Escort van, which greatly facilitated the transport of stock.

When the organisation had started in 1966, it had operated with a total annual working budget of £7,000; by 1973, from a turnover of £45,859, it achieved a commercial value of medical equipment exported to the order of £180,000.

....oOo....

12 : Blessings out of buffetings

During these early days of the development of ECHO, Marley Manor was also becoming established, but it seemed that a larger number of guests would be required to make the whole project practical. So we felt led to increase the accommodation by adding some extra bedrooms and another bathroom.

Our two daughters, Josephine and Rosemary, settled into their new schools and fitted into the routine of the Centre with much enthusiasm. A pony was added to the family menagerie and this created riding interests, which resulted in an annual gymkhana in aid of the R.S.P.C.A. and Fauna Preservation Society, also one or two animal lovers' services. These events were entirely organised by the girls, who obviously inherited their parents' organising abilities!

We now established an annual 'Open Day' and this brought many friends and house-guests together. The Chapel was greatly used by many people; regular Sunday evening services were held in the summer months, daily evening devotions, Holy Communion and special services at Christmas and Easter.

In 1966 we became involved in the Greater London Crusade, led by Dr. Billy Graham, at Earls Court in London, and had the joy of seeing young lives transformed by personal commitment to Jesus Christ.

We needed a large centre to follow up these young Christians and decided to hold the first of a series of 'Follow-up Squashes' at Marley Manor, and invited the Rev. Douglas C. Sparks, the European, Middle East and African Director of 'The Navigators', to address the Squash. Several young people came to the Lord on this occasion, and we began to realise how this Centre could be used for events other than the entertainment of private guests.

We later had a request from the Billy Graham Evangelistic Association, to use Marley Manor for their counselling and training team, as they planned the nationwide closed circuit television relays for the 'All Britain Crusade' to be held in 1967. The week was a tremendous success, and as we saw the great nationwide counselling and television relays being planned from Marley

Manor, we humbly realised how God was using the Centre. Resulting from this it was our privilege to have the Billy Graham Team and staff to stay over Easter 1967 for a week's retreat prior to the Crusade. We organised over 300 people in coach parties every night for the 'All Britain Crusade' at Earls Court, and Marley Manor became the evangelical centre for three-monthly reunion inter-church 'Squashes'. The Squash following the Crusade was conducted by Harvey Thomas, and about 320 people from 30 different churches packed into the house. Marley Manor was also the chosen centre for the first organised inter-church follow-up group for the 14-25-year-olds, and an active youth group started meeting every Sunday afternoon. There were other activities too and Christmas 1967 the young people produced a floodlit Nativity Pageant on Lion Green, Haslemere, complete with donkey, sheep and Kings' horses (instead of camels!). The whole presentation was mimed by 30-40 young people and recorded over sound relay equipment. This presentation was repeated for three years.

There were several family casualties in 1967, as once more the Lord led us through the valley of trial and testing. James broke his wrist whilst ice-skating with the girls at Brighton, and Josephine developed appendicitis on an overnight mountain trek at Crusader Camp in Italy, and had to be rushed to Turin for surgery. Then, soon after all this, we had a further serious crisis whilst on holiday with the family in Malta. Quite suddenly Rosemary was rushed to Valletta Hospital with an acute attack of paratyphoid. She was desperately ill and on continuous intravenous fluids for four days as her life hung in the balance. I think we were too stunned to realise how disastrous this might have been. We sent urgent messages to our home church (at that time Farnham Baptist Church) for prayer on her behalf. Then quite dramatically one morning, when a surgeon had been called in, Rosemary turned the corner and even the Methodist Minister who so faithfully stayed with her through this critical period, could hardly believe what he saw as the screens were removed and Rosemary smiled the most relaxed smile we had seen in days. It was not until we got home that we discovered this was the very morning that news had reached faithful Christian friends at home, who were at that very moment on their knees in prayer. Then people say that they do not believe in miracles and prayer! It is when we are so desperate and so dependant upon God at a time like this, that His love is more precious than anything else on earth and yet it is so easy to forget, and to return to our carefree way of life with our limited 'organised' times with the Lord. In His mercy and love He forgives and forgets our waywardness and how much we owe our praises and thanks, for we are so unworthy of His loving care and concern.

But our lives seemed to have been continually fraught with ups and downs. Moments of thrill and excitement; moment of anxiety and pain, moments of unexpected happenings.

As the work of Marley Manor developed and an increasing number of people began to use the Centre, our little chapel - known as 'The Chapel on the Hill' - became too small. As we prayed about it, we felt our next development at Marley Manor should be the extension of the Chapel, not only to accommodate larger numbers, but also to incorporate a quiet reading room and a room to house our extensive Congo museum. The quiet room would enable people to read or study and there would be a smaller plate glass picture window looking out over the valley and the Chapel garden. The museum would be dedicated to missionaries who laid down their lives for Christ in the Congo uprisings.

So, on May 11th, 1968, the building was complete and we were thrilled at the new enlarged Chapel, completely carpeted and with full electric heating and lighting; it was indeed a worthy House of God.

The Chapel on the hill, Marley Manor

The Chapel extension was officially opened and dedicated by the late Rev. J. C. Rendall, MA, a great friend of Kathleen Hasler and ex-Minister of the Baptist Church in Harrow, where we were married and from which we were sent as missionaries to the Congo.

The museum extension was dedicated by the late Sir Clement C. Chesterman OBE, MD, FRCP, who had played such an important part as a medical missionary in the control of sleeping sickness in the Congo. Many of his own exhibits were in the museum.

Mr. D. W. Truby, representing the Unevangelised Fields Mission, so many of whose missionaries were martyred in the Congo uprisings, spoke at a most moving Memorial Service which was led by Rev. Cyril H. Chilvers, Pastor of Farnham Baptist Church. Missionaries and representatives of many Missionary Societies were present, and even the enlarged Chapel would not hold all those who joined us for the Dedication and Memorial Service.

We little realised when we first met members of the British staff of the Navigators in February 1967, what a far-reaching effect this would have on the work and ministry of Marley Manor. Through links with the work of this organisation was to begin a new chapter in the work of the Centre. 'The Navigators' is an international, interdenominational Christian organisation, and their objective is to make disciples of all nations.

We held our first Student House party over Easter 1968, led by a young Navigator. This was a time of tremendous blessing and two young people came to know the Lord. To our utter joy, one of these was our own daughter, Rosemary.

Student House parties now became a regular feature of the new era and led to the national and regional European Staff Conference of the Navigators. During the summer of 1970, we welcomed our most ambitious Conference, a Navigator Training and Work Camp. These groups held in centres around Great Britain were designed as Basic Training Camps for young Christians, and after a morning of study, the 'Gang' went to work and for five hours the grounds hummed with activity. During the week many outside maintenance jobs were done, including the painting of the house and Chapel. Each evening we joined in fellowship with these fine Christian friends and we were truly sorry when the end of the really happy week arrived.

More and more, Marley Manor was now being used by Conference groups and we began to realise its potential in God's service as a small evangelical Conference and Holiday Centre. In the spring of 1970 we had held a Conference of the Leaders of the Mid-Wessex Christian Camps and catered for 40 guests! Twenty had to be accommodated out of the house! We were finding the Centre was becoming increasingly difficult to run financially, with costs rising all the time, and yet we were being challenged to go forward with a whole new programme of development! As we prayed about the future of Marley Manor and its usefulness for the Lord, surprising plans were born as we discussed the future of the Centre with experienced and wise Christian advisors.

There grew in our hearts the conviction that God was calling us forward into a whole new venture of faith. Already our legal advisors were suggesting the time would soon come when Marley Manor should become a registered charitable Trust, and a whole new exciting future seemed to lay ahead of us as the 'Friends of Marley Manor' scheme was born.

Apart from extra accommodation, the facilities really needed were a swimming-pool, garden and indoor games centre, a coffee lounge, a bookstall for Christian literature and an extension of the facilities for the very popular sport of horse riding. During the winter of 1970-1971 work began on two house extensions to incorporate a coffee bar and another lounge, a games hut and a large modern heated and filtered swimming pool, with the necessary changing rooms.

On Saturday, March 6th, 1971, a voluntary team of students from King Edward's School Christian Union, Southampton, arrived to start digging the new swimming pool with the help of a JCB mechanical digger and two 'dumper trucks' and 'Operation Swimming Pool' began.

Just when we were rejoicing and praising the Lord for the thrill of this fantastic project, tragedy involved us and disrupted all our excitement. Rosemary was now studying at the College of Education in Doncaster. One Sunday morning she phoned us to say that the two friends with whom she shared 'digs' had been killed in a car crash. We dropped everything and rushed up the M1 to Doncaster. It was a sad visit to say the least. Apparently the two students and two other friends had asked Rosemary to join them; they planned to visit the college for a social evening on the Saturday night, but Rosemary was not really interested and declined the offer. Their car and a bus met on one of the country lanes; the bus ploughed into the car and all four students were killed. It was a terrible shock to Rosemary in particular, and indeed to us all, and how we thanked God for yet another wonderful revelation of His care and protection over our beloved daughter. Our hearts went out to the other parents; we too might have been in their situation and this made our love and concern for them even greater. We prayed so much that the peace and comfort of Jesus would be theirs at this time. Rosemary's shock was not improved by the fact that, in the early hours of the Sunday morning, as she and the landlady were anxiously waiting to know why the girls had not returned, the police came to break the news and asked them to go to the hospital to identify the bodies. It had a profound effect upon her. She came straight home with us, only to be called back the next day to attend the inquest. The following week she went to stay with Navigators friends in Finland to get right away from everyone. The beautiful winter weather and sympathetic friends in Finland helped Rosemary to overcome what had been a very severe shock. This emergency visit to Finland, however, led eventually to her future marriage and a period of missionary work in that land.

When Rosemary returned, we were just starting the swimming pool project and it helped to take her mind off things as she plunged in to help me with the immense task of feeding the work force that descended upon us!

The first Navigator work team of University and College students moved in. We were about to attempt a highly technical construction job to build a modern luxury swimming pool. The firm told us the minimum time for construction would be eight weeks. We were to attempt it with student volunteer labour in just two weeks!

By the time the Navigator Work Camp students left, they had achieved the 'near impossible', and the major part of the building and installation work was completed. The professionals moved in as the work parties left, and finished the pool lining with marble chips and mosaic tiles and laid the paving stone surrounds, and 'Operation Swimming Pool' was completed.

On the afternoon of Saturday, May 22nd, 1971, the swimming pool was officially dedicated and opened at our annual 'Open Day', to be used in the work here to the Glory of God and the enjoyment of many people.

In 1971 some of our most successful conferences gave us the joy of seeing people of all ages committing their lives to Jesus Christ. In a relaxed holiday atmosphere, the living Christ became very real to many people. Two of the most popular conferences were, 'Problems of relating Science and Scripture', led by Rev. David Pawson, and the 'Music Week', led by Mr. Tim Buckley and his talented musical family. At this latter, members of the conference were fitted into a programme according to their talent and, after only five days of practice, a concert was produced at St. Christopher's Church, Haslemere, which was a great success and a great blessing to the packed audience in the Church. During the conference, the new facilities were used to the full, particularly the swimming pool, tennis, table tennis and other garden games. Riding requests led us to purchase another horse.

It was during 1973 that we began to realise that the pressure of work both at ECHO and at Marley Manor, together with other medical commitments, was becoming more than we could efficiently manage. We could not carry on developing both organisations; it was obvious that either we must put all our efforts into the work at Marley Manor , or put all our efforts into ECHO.

In June we went to Israel with a party from our home Church and it was during this time we were able to consider the Lord's will for our future service. Somehow we felt we could not consider dropping the responsibilities of Marley Manor, and we contemplated the possibilities of handing over ECHO. It would be essential for James to give more time at home when we had these bigger conference groups, but it was obvious that he could not be in two places at once. These were our thoughts as we left for Israel. The Lord was very near to us as we prayed about the whole situation so close to the places He himself had visited.

On our return, we were still hesitant as to the correct decision to make, but at the same time we began to feel much more certain that ECHO needed us. God never leaves a prayer unanswered. He may have to correct, test and prove us first, but in His own time the answer comes, and we need always to be on the alert to discern His guidance. Nevertheless, when a spectacular answer is revealed, we generally show signs of surprise. I suppose this is because, human nature being what it is, we often pray for things which seem impossible, failing to realise that if God wants a certain situation, then not even a mountain can stand in the way. We should not be surprised when God answers our prayers, but full of praise because He has revealed His love and concern.

So it was that we returned to England to sort out the business of two week's absence and news from ECHO brought a startling confirmation of God's will for our future. A large, anonymous bank draft for £25,000 had been received at ECHO headquarters, earmarked 'For the development of ECHO'. What a confirmation! Little did the donor realise how great he or she was being used in answering a desperate prayer.

From that moment we had no doubts. Two weeks before, we could not consider a move from Marley Manor; the call to take up that work had been so clear at the time, just as our call to Africa had been in earlier years, but God has His plans all ready laid, and often they may include a change in the whole direction of a life committed to Him. The important thing is to be flexible in the hands of the Lord, prepared and willing to change course if this is what He wants us to do.

Immediately, our outlook had to be re-directed and we considered the vast mission field ahead of us in the expanding and developing work of ECHO. James now offered to serve in full-time capacity, to cope with increasing demands. As soon as Marley Manor was sold and a smaller house obtained, there would be no need for time to be spent in the running of a busy Conference Centre. But we were very soon to realise that we still had many more lessons to learn. There was a sudden slump in the property market, and we fell right into it; Marley Manor just would not sell. We had to learn lessons in patience and frustration and realise our complete and utter dependence upon the Lord, in the confidence that He had the whole situation under control. It's easy to say one feels this way, but only a daily filling of the Holy Spirit and a total love for Jesus could keep us in an attitude of calm assurance and praise.

....oOo....

13 : More cloudy valleys

Suddenly, everything seemed to be tumbling around us. We were confident that God had a plan and purpose in the testing and training through which we were passing, but I suppose it is only natural to become frustrated on the human level in a situation like this and we were no exception to the rule. We realised, too, that experience and obedience go hand in hand, and that patience and trust had to be learnt before the Lord could release us for the further period of service for which He was preparing us. So we began to praise the Lord for the mere fact of being chosen for this training at all.

It became increasingly difficult to maintain Marley Manor financially as the months dragged on. This, perhaps, was one of the greatest strains, and we were very conscious that Satan was trying to break us at this point; we were so conscious, too, of the prayers of many, as they uplifted us so much.

Eventually, we had to take some kind of action and, after two and a half years, we were advised to take the property off the market and apply to the Council for a change of usage of the Centre, to a registered Nursing Home. Formalities went through without difficulty and thus we plunged into a period of upheavals and chaos, as necessary structural requirements had to be carried out.

To keep costs down, we agreed to carry out the work ourselves with private, professional and amateur help, rather than hand over the work to a firm. We did not realise what we were undertaking and, apart from a brief break for Christmas, structural alterations carried on from early November 1975 until March 1976, followed by a massive decoration programme, cleaning and repairing curtains and carpets, sorting stock, etc. Over half a mile of cable alone, together with hundreds of yards of wiring was laid, necessitating the removal of many floorboards. All rooms were affected in one way or another, for the installation of smoke detectors, heat detectors, alarm bells, emergency lighting, and call bells for each bed. Twenty-six doors had to be checked for weight, fire-proofed and fixed with automatic closing devices; some had to be backed with asbestos. The central oak staircase had to be closed in with fireproof panelling and glass, and an electrically operated door positioned at the top of the staircase.

There were other structural alterations to be made and the addition of further basins, baths and toilet facilities, which involved drilling up part of the tarmac drive. The whole operation was not easy and we were very conscious of strain and tension through the continued chaos, noise and mess day after day, week after week. But we were conscious, too, of strength and endurance, obviously God-given, in the midst of the whole situation, as a tremendous answer to the prayers of so many over the past year or two, began to emerge.

Thus we moved ourselves to a new house in Haslemere, and a Matron took over the running of the Home. We had already started taking the first patients before we moved. Later on, we had the opportunity to dispose of the Home altogether, in order to give all our time and concentration to ECHO.

Throughout all these busy years at Marley Manor, strength in abundance had returned to me following the original heart condition I had when we left Africa. Indeed, the Lord had healed and restored me and showered us all with so many blessings. Gradually, I slipped back into a normal routine of activity with as much vigour as I had previously experienced. But there are times when we can be too active and too enthusiastic, so that people admire our ability to cope with so much, and one feels a sense of elevation and even pride. In order to curb this situation, the Lord sometimes has to deal firmly with us. If we ignore the warnings He sets before us, sometimes through conscience, through the Word of God, or maybe through the words of someone else, then He has to take further steps. Because I would not listen to reason, I had to learn the hard way and bear the consequences this involved. We knew too, that Satan and his evil powers were not at all happy with the way ECHO was developing in the service of the Lord, and maybe he was intervening in an attempt to dishearten us. How do we discern these things?

Whatever the reason, this is how I was to accept the third major physical crisis in my life. I was rejoicing in the joys of a happy, busy and fulfilling life, lashing my abilities in every direction; involvement with ECHO, caring for people in our guest and conference centre, riding and swimming every day, involving myself with the family and all their activities, taking on a fair share of the necessary gardening and care of the grounds, and trying to fit God in between. My priorities were all out of order, with my Bible study and prayer times undisciplined and my work programme taking the lead. Warning signs simply passed me by until one day, visiting the hospital for a routine gynae check, a small tumour was detected. I was stunned; I felt well enough and could not accept that anything could possibly be wrong or that this was really happening to me. I certainly did not fancy abdominal surgery, which seemed to be the main topic of the conversation. But, like it or not, five days later I was on the operating table having a generous portion of my interior removed! As if that was not enough, a few days later acute sepsis set in and I lay in a pretty sorry state. I gave up trying to understand what was happening.

This was all at the time when, as mentioned previously, we were experiencing increasing difficulties with Marley Manor; in fact, it was actually during the time we were trying to sell the property. So James had a double anxiety situation to cope with, and needed an abundant portion of physical strength and spiritual faith to shoulder all this, plus the increasing demands of ECHO. It was not an easy time for him and I felt so helpless to support him in it all.

So once more I came back to God to seek His forgiveness for my waywardness and to rededicate my life to Him. If He could further use me, I would give every ounce of myself to Him and have faith that healing would take place. I thought positively and God in His love and grace generously accepted my plea, and I was completely healed. There was no dramatic miracle; it took a long time, with several minor crises along the way, but in the end I felt good and I was soon raring to go again. Well, after all, hadn't I promised to give the Lord every ounce of myself if He healed me?

Don't ever think you are superhuman! Maybe some folk can do more than others but we are all basically human beings and, as Christians, our bodies are temples of the Holy Spirit and, as such, we should respect them and consider them with care. But I have always had difficulty in 'being still', impatient by nature, and having an active mind that is always creating and scheming; it was not easy to consider doing things in a quiet, dignified way!

Nevertheless, we once more settled down to a routine in our new home. We enjoyed entertaining, and were surrounded by beautiful country. We had a pleasant garden of reasonable proportions and this was a source of outlet for excess of energy and also a place of relaxation and rest; not least was the enjoyment others seemed to receive from its beauty. We had been sad when our horses had to go from Marley Manor; now we had a Welsh mountain pony Stud at the end of the garden and enjoyed watching their activities. How good is the God we adore; He understood our pleasures and saw to it that we were not completely cut off from them!

Life was now quieter than of late and ran smoothly for a while, apart from the odd family experiences that happen to us all from time to time.

Our eldest daughter, Josephine, had been married in 1971 while we were still at Marley Manor and by now we had our first grand-child, Ruth, who was a real joy to us. Seven years later Josephine and Mike had a son, Timothy, but had fostered 14 other young children and babies in between. Josephine certainly put her Great Ormond Street training into practice.

Now, Rosemary, returning from a teaching post in Finland, was to be married. Not content with the normal run of things, she had to have a carriage and pair to keep in with her 'horsey' trends. After a brief honeymoon, the happy couple returned to Finland to take up duties in the Navigator ministry in that country which, by now, they both knew very well and were able to speak the language fluently. Two years later, Gareth was born and we had the opportunity to visit Finland to be with the family for a brief stay. We were impressed by the peace and tranquillity of Finland, the lakes and the forests and the attractive farmlands. One week of this visit was spent together in a little log cabin by the lakeside; a lazy week resting by the quiet waters, boating, fishing, walking through the woods, swimming, 'sauna-ing' and enjoying barbecue suppers. Mod cons were a thing of the unknown; we even had to wash in the lake! Back at Jyvaskyla we met some of the fellows and girls from the university who were involved in the Navigator Bible study groups which were supervised by Roger and Rosemary. They testified how they had come to know Jesus Christ and were now witnessing to others about their faith. We praised God for the involvement that our daughter and son-in-law had, and for their devotion to the Lord. Two years later their daughter, Laura was born.

Having settled down, I now began to look for an outlet for my restless 'spirit'. I formed a ladies Bible study group which flourished week by week from the start and was a great blessing to many ladies from a number of different churches in the Haslemere area. I got involved with our church choir and joined the missionary committee, also visiting ECHO once a week to become more closely involved with the audio-visual department. Things were hotting up again and I was in my element!

Then, quite suddenly, after four happy years at our new home, we felt quite certain that the Lord was asking us to move once more. A number of factors brought this step about but we knew it was the right decision and we felt a wonderful peace about the whole situation. Thus we rented another house in Haslemere for a while. It was quite miraculous how dates, transactions, etc., all fitted in, which we were sure could only mean that, having been obedient to this 'command' from the Lord, His hand was upon it all.

Once more, burying ourselves in packing boxes, everything seemed on schedule when, like a bolt out of the blue, another crisis situation confronted us. James was rushed into hospital for emergency surgery to remove a kidney stone. This happened to coincide with the week of our move but, as always, the Lord enabled us to face up to the situation with the necessary extra strength and fortitude needed at times like this. James suffered a great deal of discomfort and pain over the initial period and, of course, was right out of action for the actual move.

Nevertheless, with the aid of many kind friends I managed to supervise things and we soon settled into our rented home to which James eventually returned for a period of convalescence. Here we were to remain for a further three and a half years until we found an ideal home back on the common, near to Marley Manor where we had spent 14 very happy and busy years.

....oOo....

14 : ECHO advances

In 1974 ECHO launched out into a wealth of new ideas and developments. The Medical and Administrative Directors (James and Bill Davies) now headed a staff of over 20 members.

There were trained nurses for selecting and sorting equipment, a task that only medically trained personnel could do adequately; trained packers, trained maintenance men, warehousing staff, administrative and secretarial staff. All were united in the task of running ECHO, and the staff continued to grow as the organisation developed in response to increasing world-wide demand.

A comprehensive catalogue of 2,000 different instruments and items of modern medical equipment available to customers was published. New storage and display techniques were used, so that the warehouse was classified according to the catalogue, thus greatly facilitating the assembly of orders. The organisation was now serving one third of the 2,000 missionary and charitable hospitals, in seventy-eight different countries throughout the world.

As a further service to missions, ECHO developed its own shipping department. This involved specialist staff and the preparation of many copies of shipping papers; there was Marine Insurance to be organised, shipping space to be booked and consignments to be delivered to the docks on the due dates. This was a very big task, as over 500 major shipments were at this time being shipped during the space of one year. There were also shipping rebates to obtain from shipping firms. Then we began to help missionary societies by undertaking the shipping of items other than medical equipment - Bibles to Zaire for the Bible Society, Land Rover parts for another mission, and various other items as the need arose, including missionaries' personal belongings and baggage. The services of ECHO were beginning to enable missionary funds to be released for the direct work of spreading the Gospel.

As we became more and more independent and established, and as turnover increased, prices were kept down and even reduced. Already, dramatic savings were being achieved for mission hospitals and medical relief programmes by taking advantage of the bulk buying of goods. Many instruments costing £3-£4 each were being supplied from ECHO's stocks for as little as 50p. More sophisticated equipment such as major surgical diathermy units, anaesthetic machines and reconditioned x-ray units were able to be supplied at one quarter to one third of normal costs, thus saving hundreds or indeed thousands of pounds of medical missionary money.

ECHO's policy was always to sell equipment at cost, plus renovating, handling, packing and freight charges. (Even so, most equipment could be supplied at between one quarter and one half of the normal commercial price.) Now, in order to overcome the escalating costs of packing materials and the service rendered by packing sub-contractors, it became possible to purchase bulk quantities of Tri-Wall boxes at reduced prices. This development led to the commencement of our own final packing department, which resulted in ultimate savings to receiving hospitals and further reduction in the delay in the processing of orders.

The preparation of heavy export crates was a major factor in making costs escalate even more, so ECHO took on the task of making its own crates, buying in timber by the cubic metre, and thereby saving 50% of the export packing costs.

Packing also involved padding - and even this could be put to good use, for the recipients were able to use the foam rubber to make into pillows. They could also use the wooden crates to make a variety of things.

We were still able to make dramatic special purchase savings: as when 17,500 sterile blood administration sets were purchased for £350, where previously they had been bought for £1 a set! But, as time went on, it became difficult to obtain secondhand or redundant equipment and we had to consider moving into the field of bulk purchasing and buying at large sales, thus obtaining greatly increased savings. To do this, we would need a lot more space than we had at Sutton. Already we were renting warehouses in five different areas, which was proving very impractical and costly. It was going to be necessary to look for yet another centre, which would need to be even bigger than Sutton.

The Administrators visited twenty-two potentially suitable premises or sites and contacted numerous agents, between Wimbledon and Chichester. At the next committee meeting, there was unanimous agreement to go ahead with the renting of an excellent new building in a new industrial area at Chichester, Sussex; 10,000 square feet, at a rent of approximately £7,500 per annum (76p a square foot), much less than similar accommodation in the London area. Now all the stock could be moved from the other warehouses to be centralised under one roof. This operation took two months, with 40-foot articulated lorries arriving most days. There were several hundred tons of stock to house and every available inch of the new warehouse was needed. The final load arrived during the last week in February, 1974. The whole operation cost well over £1,000 in transport costs alone.

This centre at Chichester was to be used as a bulk store and for the intake and sorting or scrapping of all incoming equipment. The large ECHO transport was to be based at Chichester, and weekly deliveries made to Sutton to supply outgoing orders. The value of our stock now amounted to hundreds of thousands of pounds; in fact, we now had a bigger supply of instruments in stock than most other surgical instrument firms in the United Kingdom, carrying a stock of 600,000 surgical instruments of all types: and all to be used for the advantage of our missionary colleagues and for disaster calls to our many member missions and relief agencies.

Day-to-day expenses and routine overhead costs were met by a very small mark-up on goods, and the vast majority of the enormous savings created by bulk purchasing were passed on to the missions and organisations we served. It has always been the policy of ECHO not to divert to the organisation those funds normally given by the public to their own specific charity or missionary interest and for ECHO to become a self-supporting missionary organisation.

Early in 1975 we were offered the other half of the Chichester premises, a building of the same dimensions; a further 10,000 square feet of modern warehousing and offices. This was considered a possible opportunity for the future, and we praised the Lord that a Christian warehousing firm came forward and agreed to hold and use the building until such time as it might be possible for ECHO to move the total operation from the expensive Sutton area, if this proved the right step. As events developed, however, the rapid expansion of ECHO was shortly to necessitate a move from Sutton to even larger premises, and it was considered wise to close the Chichester warehouse and not accept this further offer, and to centralise the whole operation under one roof in the future, to minimise overhead costs.

At the Filey Christian Holiday Crusade of the same year, we exhibited a fully-equipped operating theatre complete with dummy patient, blood drip, cardiac monitor, diathermy unit, instruments, theatre furniture, etc. The idea was to illustrate the overall cost saving to missions and charities by our work. As a result, the interest shown in the work of ECHO took off like a rocket and we made many helpful contacts.

This publicity led to a busy deputation programme during the coming winter months, visiting churches and groups throughout the country with transparencies and display panels. The story of the development of ECHO was widely shared and a number of the staff united in the deputation programme. This outreach was very rewarding, not least in terms of interest and encouragement; though financially, too, we were delighted at the response. A Trustee of a big charitable Trust was present at a certain Sheffield deputation meeting. He was so thrilled with the film presentation of the story of ECHO that he approached his Trust and a grant of £5,000 was sent to ECHO a few weeks later. An interested nurse, on another occasion, received back pay of £30 from the National Health Service. She sent this as a gift to help the work of ECHO. Another girl present at Filey had saved £500 for her college training. When she received an unexpected grant to help her college expenses, she sent the £500 as a gift to ECHO. Specially designed collecting boxes also brought an extra income of gifts.

Every week gifts arrived in the post, each one precious in the Lord's eyes for, great or small, these were love gifts from people who wanted to share in the ministry of providing urgently required medical needs throughout remote areas of the world. Sometimes, medical firms sent gifts in kind or sold us stock at nominal prices.

All were to be sent out and used in medical mission and relief work; all were given in the Name of Jesus and for His sake. The Bible says *(Isaiah 58:10 Living Bible)* *'Feed the hungry! Help those in trouble! Then your light will shine out from the darkness, and the darkness around you shall be as bright as day.'*

Having been commissioned by the C.B.M.S. Committee in 1967 to develop a joint missionary medical equipment service, we returned to this same Committee in May 1975, eight years later to report what had already been achieved and, as world inflation posed some of the most acute problems ever faced by medical missions, to share with them the challenge that the Council of ECHO had taken up.

No-one on the C.B.M.S. Committee in 1967 ever thought that the small organisation - created to take advantage of the surplus hospital supplies then available due to hospital rebuilding, and envisaged initially as a two-year short-term operation - would have evolved eight years later into a major enterprise. It now carried a specialised staff of over twenty members and was supplying nearly 800 mission hospitals in 80 different countries of the world, as well as many disaster and medical relief programmes overseas. We never imagined in those early days an organisation carrying a larger stock of medical equipment and supplies than many commercial medical equipment firms.

By 1975 ECHO had shipped or air-freighted more than 3,000 consignments round the world and had become an organisation working internationally, serving missions from practically every country in the Western World and very many national Christian organisations, Protestant and Catholic alike. We never realised, either, that the initial annual budget of £7,000 - half of which was given by member missions and the rest by Christian Aid and Oxfam - would increase to a budget of £260,000 in 1976, making ECHO a self-supporting venture. By the end of 1974, at a cost of £263,000, ECHO had supplied medical equipment to a commercial value of £1,051,000 - a total saving to medical missionary causes of £788,000 - from an initial two-year grant support of £3500 per annum from C.B.M.S. members. This was an investment of missionary money paying tremendous dividends.

During 1976, in consultation with the World Health Organisation in Geneva, ECHO was involved with the development of Rural Health Centres and Village Clinics. The Rural Health Centres were to be sited within rural communities and would be controlled by regional hospitals within the nearer urban centre. This programme was aimed to assist the desperate need for rural health care in poorer nations overseas. The Health Centres and Village Clinics would all be staffed by adequately trained personnel.

The Rural Health Centre consisted of a treatment room, examination room, minor operating room, obstetrics and gynaecological room and a rural health laboratory, all being divided into five self-contained units. The whole Centre was equipped at a cost of approximately £1,500.

From the Rural Health Centres, a wide area of villages was covered by a network of small Village Clinics. These Clinics were produced and packed for export for approximately £325, including a microscope and basic equipment requirements. These were prepared by ECHO in advance so that they were ready at a moment's notice for immediate despatch. The prices have risen a little over the years but are still very nominal compared with commercial prices.

One of the highlights of 1977 was a visit to the Sutton Headquarters of H.R.H. Princess Alexandra. Her Royal Highness displayed a keen interest throughout her tour and was particularly interested in the Rural Health Centre and Village Clinic kits.

In 1978, in an effort to meet the need of high-quality, low-priced medical and surgical equipment for mission hospitals, ECHO introduced its own range of hospital furniture to its own specification. These were now manufactured in quantity by engineering companies under contract to ECHO. Because of ECHO's non-profit making policy, this development led to

Visit of HRH Princess Alexandra to ECHO

enormous savings in the cost of new, high-quality medical equipment. For example, a simple operating table, normally priced commercially at £1,500, was available from ECHO for £200.

All these new developments, however, meant that even the Sutton Headquarters became much too cramped for the increasing development of ECHO's work. It was necessary to search for another centre where expansion could be carried out efficiently.

At last I began to understand how God was working in our lives. If we had not been obedient in the first instance and battled through several years of training before going to Africa, probably none of this would have happened. To begin with, we would not have realised the vast scale of poverty in the Third World. On the whole, people in the Western World don't realise the appalling conditions in these situations. We see pictures and we say, 'Oh, how terrible.' We give to a fund to help in some particular crisis or situation and, for many people, that's as far as it goes.

As far as we were concerned, we were seeing the fulfilment of God's plans as ECHO launched out to meet the requirements of a desperately needy world.

15: Cheaper by the million

During 1975, hospital after hospital overseas and parent missionary organisations in the Western World asked ECHO to consider the supply of vital drugs needed to run any modern medical work. We were now well geared to supply, cheaply and effectively, all the medical equipment needs of charity hospitals throughout the world; but inflation was now imposing another problem of viability to all mission hospitals in respect of drugs. So great had been the escalation in the world cost of pharmaceuticals that many charity hospitals, working in areas of world poverty and need, could no longer remain viable. It was no use supplying equipment if the vital, life-saving drugs for their work were not available. Many international organisations were seeking to help in this field; could ECHO help the situation which was now placing an impossible burden on mission hospitals throughout the world?

Thus it was that we began a pharmaceutical research operation that was to have far-reaching effects on the future of the organisation. An initial questionnaire sent to all our member missions and Trusts showed an overwhelming concern for getting the price of vitally important drugs down to a level that charity hospitals and medical relief units could afford. It was obvious that only a co-ordinated approach through bulk buying and distribution and through special manufacturing could meet this need.

The first step was to assess the whole problem very carefully as the Council of ECHO instructed its officers to institute a research programme into every aspect of the need. A detailed survey questionnaire was sent to hundreds of overseas mission hospitals, seeking to assess whether such a bulk buying pharmaceutical service would be acceptable and supported by the hospitals. The questionnaire also sought to find out what drugs were most urgently needed and in what quantities.

The problem of an adequate supply of drugs for mission hospitals was by no means a new one. Long before ECHO came into being there were signs that the supply of drugs was becoming a major problem. The following extracts taken from news and prayer letters from missionaries give some idea of the need and highlight the problem which, over the years, was becoming increasingly more critical.

From a hospital in Zaire in 1961, a doctor wrote:

'Drugs are becoming a desperate problem - or perhaps I had better say the lack of them. For the first time we are out of TB drugs and have had to discontinue treatment on practically all our patients except those who can afford to pay for the little stock we have which we bought for emergency use. We are praying that we will be able to obtain further stocks soon...'

Also in 1961:

'Our drug supply is now getting very low. We did get some good supplies but now these are not coming in and we - a hospital in the midst of a very bad malaria area - are almost out of anti-malarial drugs; our stock of antibiotics is also very low and aspirins now completely out of stock. Our tuberculosis drugs are also running low. Will you pray that the supply will be forthcoming as we cannot buy them here and just have no money to put large orders in as we used to do.'

In 1975 the worldwide supply of drugs to mission hospitals was still critical - inflation fanned the flames created by world poverty and need. The questionnaire we circulated threw up enormous demands, especially in the basic generic life-saving drugs such as the antibiotics, the anti-leprosy drugs, the anti-tubercular drugs, the anti-malarial drugs, etc. For example, a mission on the Ivory Coast spent £15,000 on drugs in 1973; for the same amount of drugs in 1975 it spent nearly £40,000. ECHO set itself the task of reducing that expenditure to the 1973 level.

Tens of millions, indeed hundreds of millions of tablets and injections would be needed to supply the 2,000 mission and charity hospital units in the world. God had called ECHO into being to serve a world of need and, in daring even to think of meeting such a vast need as this latest development revealed, we were confident that He would enable us to tackle effectively a task which seemed impossible and unthinkable for such a small organisation.

As in the exciting days of the formation of ECHO in 1966, when the first survey revealed so much need for medical equipment everywhere, so now in 1975 the drug survey resulted in a staggering response. A representative sample of the first hundred hospitals to help in the survey not only showed a very high proportion willing and anxious to participate in a bulk-buying missionary pharmaceutical service, but revealed that a total budget of one and a half million pounds was already being spent on drugs in these one hundred hospitals. As the total of mission hospitals in the world was 2,000, this meant that the total amount spent must be nearly twenty times this figure.

Obviously, a lot more detailed research and planning would need to be carried out before we could be in a position to take such an enormous leap forward. The next few months involved a hectic programme of investigations into every aspect of the problem which included high-level discussions with pharmaceutical companies in the United Kingdom and Europe and with many Government departments and other organisations already working in the field of the supply of pharmaceuticals to overseas territories. Our Administrative and Medical Directors went out of their way to learn about every step of the production and marketing of drugs, visiting many major pharmaceutical manufacturers to see for themselves the complicated procedures involved in the tableting and processing of modern drugs.

In February 1975, guided by the results of the continuing research, the Council of Management of ECHO took a momentous step of faith in launching a pilot scheme to supply the twenty-five or so basic generic life-saving drugs that were needed to treat the main endemic diseases facing mission hospitals throughout the world. With great difficulty, our original list of many hundreds of possible drugs was cut down to this number of non-patented, non-branded drugs, capable of being manufactured cheaply in bulk under their simple chemical formula. The pilot scheme allowed detailed research to continue apace while close discussion and co-operation took place with international health organisations, such as the World Health Organisation and the World Council of Churches. Government bodies, such as the Ministry of Overseas Development and the Commonwealth Secretariat were also contacted. We felt that no stone must be left unturned if this venture was to succeed. Due to the very great interest shown in the pilot scheme, and increasing world need, it soon became obvious that this small scheme would develop into a full pharmaceutical service before very long. Within a very short time, tenders were being requested for a total of twenty-five million drugs, i.e. one million of each of the basic generic drugs.

In order to exploit to the full the enormous advantage of bulk buying and special manufacturing arrangements not only of pharmaceuticals, but also of the many consumable items such as surgeon's gloves, syringes, sutures, etc., the Council of ECHO in May 1974 had approved the setting up of a bulk buying service to charities and had proposed the setting up of a separate Trust, to be called the ECHO Development Trust (or in short E.D.T.) to raise the necessary development capital funds. Whilst the complicated legal arrangements to set up the E.D.T. were proceeded with, the member missions of ECHO were approached to help by loan or gift, with the funds necessary for the setting up of our pharmaceutical and development programme.

We were overwhelmed by the generous response of our membership, and their joint gift totalling £25,000 enabled us to make an immediate start in the setting up of a 'bulk buying pharmaceutical programme'. Members felt that this initial pace-setting gift would really be a vital investment (as the initial capital to launch ECHO nine years previously had proved), reaping a handsome dividend for their own medical work in the years of increasing difficulties ahead.

Thus the ECHO Development Trust was established by Trust Deed on the 21st July, 1975, and independently registered as a Charity. Its object was to support the development of ECHO's work and to further medical missionary endeavour and the relief of suffering worldwide. The Trustees set an enormous target of £230,000 to be raised during the succeeding years, which was a tremendous challenge for a comparatively new organisation to tackle.

All gifts to the work of ECHO were to go direct to the Development Trust for this purpose; no contributions into ECHO would be applied to the maintenance and day to day running of the organisation. These would all be covered by the swift turnover of goods. Little did we realise at the time the major role to be played in the future by this new development arm of ECHO.

Thus, with the aid of the Development Trust's activity and a strong, generous financial backing support from its member organisations, ECHO was now able to expand all its services.

ECHO now stood at the threshold of a programme which could revolutionise the future of medical missionary work in the Third World: a major breakthrough in achieving the goal of worldwide bulk supplies of generic medicines available cheaply on demand. Enormous demands were being made for the drugs so desperately needed overseas and manufacturers were stretching capacity to the limit to produce these for us. Manufacture of drugs by the millions was bringing the initially low prices even lower. The Medical Director of ECHO learnt one lesson, however, in dealing with drugs

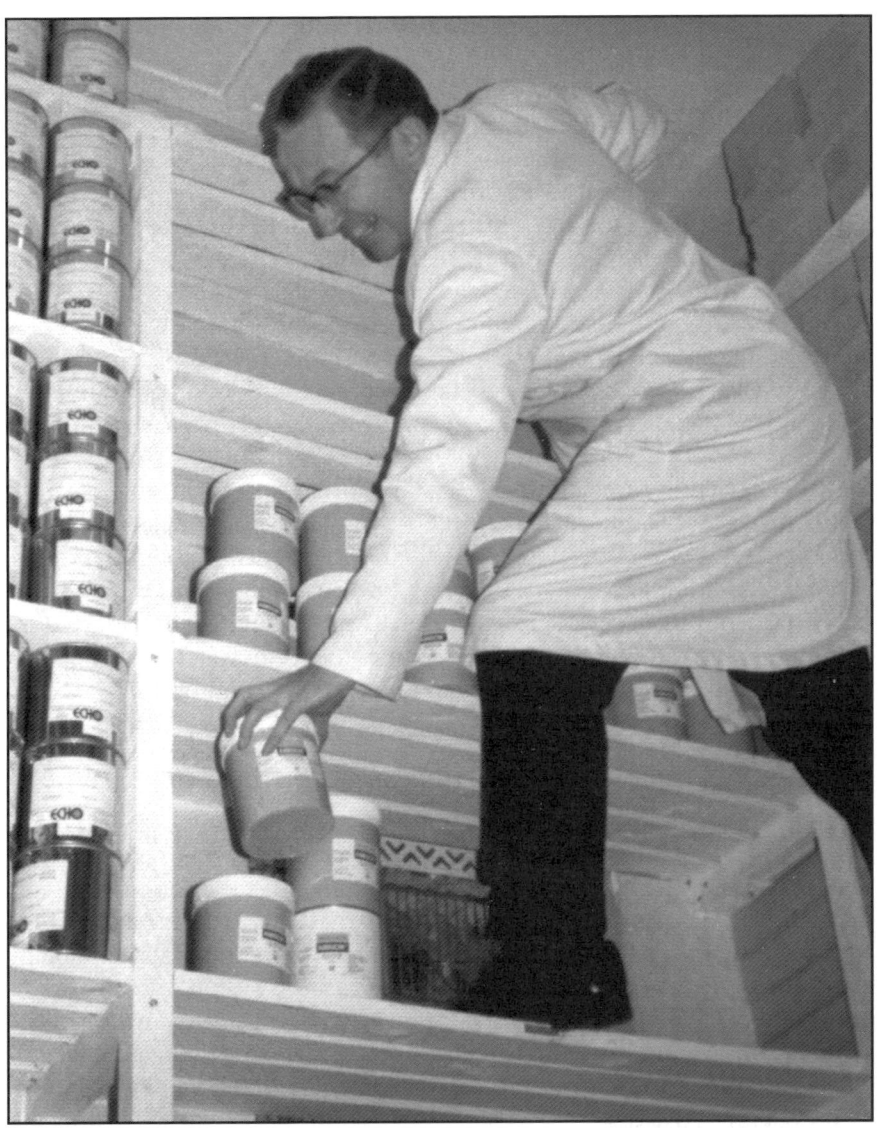

Early drug stocks

by the million! When, on one occasion, he agreed to collect one million anti-malarial tablets for an emergency airlift the next day, he went off for the consignment in the organisation's small estate car, only to discover that the order weighed eleven cwt! They packed them in but, apart from the fact that the springs of the car were completely flattened, it was no easy task to drive back through London's busy roads with no back vision and the chassis almost scraping the road surface!

A few other examples give an idea of the immensity of the task upon which ECHO had now been launched.

From the Unevangelised Fields Mission came the first order for 5,000 tablets of each of the basic generic drugs.

From Oxfam came an order for £5,000 worth of drugs to be sent out to Mozambique to meet the need in their medical services. The Portuguese Army flew them out in a special plane from Lisbon.

From the Leprosy Mission and other mission hospitals working in the leprosy field came many requests for Dapsone, causing a complete rundown of manufacturers' stocks and necessitating special production of millions of tablets for ECHO, at specially negotiated low prices, to assist leprosy treatment and eradication worldwide.

From Tear Fund came another very large order for £5,000 worth of life-saving drugs and vaccines for the 'HEED' programme in Bangladesh. Many thousands of doses of vaccines of all types were needed including measles vaccine. The latter arrived at our home on Friday night and took up the major part of our domestic refrigerator until it could be transported to Sutton for refrigeration. For this consignment, British Airways arranged to airlift the two tons of drugs free of charge for Tear Fund over a period of weeks.

From one of the West German missions came a request for over three tons of drugs for a mission hospital in the Yemen.

In April 1975 there was an urgent appeal from all the major charities for ECHO to help in the deteriorating refugee and health situation in Vietnam, necessitating the despatch of two urgent airlifts of drugs and supplies. Nearly a ton of drugs in the form of over one million anti-malarial tablets, 250,000 anti-dysentery tablets, 200,000 aspirins and 50,000 of many other basic generic drugs was sent. All this, together with intra-venous fluids, several thousand syringes and needles, blood administration sets, bandages, elastoplast, dressings, scissors, probes, forceps, scalpels and sutures made up an order of nearly £5,000.

This order had to be collected and packed within 24 hours. We heard that, at a certain drug factory, the girls working there were so shocked by the appalling conditions in Vietnam and the fact they could be involved in some helpful way that they worked right through their lunch break packing for ECHO, and also took a collection amounting to £20. The Directors of the firm doubled this, making a gift of £40 for the work of ECHO.

From a hospital in Nigeria came an urgent request for drug supplies to be sent by parcel post, because of dock strikes which would involve great delays. Forty-six parcels weighing twenty-two pounds each were sent off on that consignment - nearly half a ton of parcels!

At the beginning of 1976 ECHO was asked by the World Health Organisation to submit a report to attract the attention of authorities concerned with health care programmes in developing countries. The report briefly outlined the background of ECHO, how it operated and its plans for the future. Mention was also made of the bulk supply of pharmaceuticals and how the 'Million scheme' - launched in October 1975 - had created a saving of some 45% on original prices. A basic stock of generic medicines readily available at rock bottom prices had done much to alleviate suffering and medical inadequacies, which were intensified by a worldwide spiral in the cost of all pharmaceutical products.

It now became increasingly apparent that ECHO had a major role ahead in supplying a comprehensive range of generic drugs suitable to treat all the endemic diseases round the world, as well as by assisting missionary doctors and pharmacists in obtaining special drugs when required.

But even at this stage we never dreamt that one day ECHO would have its own highly qualified Pharmacist and Pharmaceutical Department and be organising a multi-million pound programme of generic pharmaceutical supplies to the Third World.

By 1977 the ECHO bulk pharmaceutical service was in full swing and in an act of faith a budget of £224,000 for drugs was launched. Month after month the graph of drug consignments was closely watched and by April the budget line was passed. The graph rose to £275,000 by the end of that year.

The pharmaceutical service continued to develop rapidly in 1978. Stocks of millions of tablets, capsules , ampoules, vials and bottles were piling up on shelves and space in the small Sutton warehouse became desperately short. To store bulk stocks and to stack completed consignments awaiting export became an increasing problem.

As more and more mission hospitals began to depend on ECHO for their orders, an ambitious budget of £402,000 was decided upon for 1978 for the pharmaceutical programme. This would involve the packing of many millions of drugs which would weigh hundreds of tons. Very large orders were placed with manufactureinning to recognise ECHO as a major buyer of pharmaceuticals. Orders of up to 25 million units of a product were necessary to meet increasing demands from hard-pressed hospitals overseas for high-quality, low-priced generic drugs. We were now able to ask for our own labelling on our products, as ECHO became a major pharmaceutical supplier to missionary and charity hospitals in practically every country of the developing world, with a much wider selection of essential drugs, recommended by the World Health Organisation for developing countries.

Right from the start it was evident that if ECHO was to be used to the full, then co-operation with other organisations in Europe supplying missions overseas would be necessary. Trips were, therefore, made to Denmark, Holland and West Germany to forge close ties of co-operation. By joint purchasing with other European organisations, ECHO could achieve even better prices for mission hospitals, due to the sheer size of the orders.

As more and more orders were packed in the early months of 1978, the target line was again crossed in April, as it had been in 1977. The impetus continued and by the end of the year drug consignments to the value of £518,000 had been sent to over 1,000 hospitals in 88 countries overseas. The 'impossible' had been achieved again as, once more, ECHO had responded to world need.

....oOo....

16: Bursting at the seams

By the end of 1978 we had totally outgrown our small Sutton headquarters and an end to our search for new, enlarged premises was at hand. For some years we had been looking for suitable accomodation; James and Bill had seen dozens of unsuitable premises. Then they came to Ewell and, after several visits to assess the possibilities, they decided that with some alterations this would be ideal, at least for the next few years. There was 18,500 square feet of working space, compared with 8,000 at Sutton, and this was a great improvement.

We had possession on December 1st, 1978, and that left just six weeks to get the building ready. An army of workmen moved in: central heating engineers, plumbers, carpenters, flooring and roofing specialists. New floors had be laid, new offices had to be constructed, there were repairs to be made on the roof, central heating to install, decorating and painting to be done. It was like a beehive, except that bees don't stop and contractors do! Our staff joined in, often working alongside the contractors and, in this way, we did much of the work ourselves and were able to cut down costs.

There were 320 tons of stocks and equipment to be shifted and, again to keep down the costs, we decided to tackle the move ourselves. We hired two 3-ton lorries and we also used our own transport. The driving was shared between the staff, but it was no joke in the appalling weather conditions experienced during the winter of 1978-79. The snow and ice caused frightening experiences as the heavy lorries skidded backwards and forwards over frozen roads, and sometimes through freezing fog.

As each load arrived at the new headquarters, it was deposited in the large warehouse area to be sorted. This was easier as we now had a fork-lift truck, but the chaos was unbelievable as the volume of boxes grew and often got mixed up with the workmen's paraphernalia.

The male staff worked all day, and then stayed on in the evenings and at the weekend to urge forward the operation. It was quite beyond the regular workmen to fathom out why those crazy ECHO folks had such a hunger for work.

One day, as James skidded to a halt with one of the big lorries, a short, stocky fellow engaged in the painting firm happened to be passing through the forecourt. When James jumped gaily out of the cab the painter stopped, put both hands on his hips and exclaimed, 'Cor...! It comes to something when the bosses have to drive the bloomin' lorry!'

James replied casually, 'Oh, that's no problem; we all like to join in the fun, you know'.

The poor painter recovered from his shock and carried on through the doorway wondering, no doubt, what he was going to see 'the bosses doing next. 'Some people's idea of fun!' he muttered as he dabbed his brush into the paint pot.

The staff worked together as one, and a real team spirit existed between them. Their thoughts were on the mission field overseas where millions waited for the help that ECHO could give them. It was vital that production should stop for only one week, just to cater for the main bulk of the move. Drugs had to be moved independently and it was necessary to ensure full security all along the line. A store for the Scheduled Drugs (those needing special security) was created from one special part of the new premises. It was a small area with solid steel walls and a concrete roof, and had been used during the war to store the engines for Spitfires - a bomb-proof, thief-proof structure which was absolutely ideal for drugs, with a large packing area directly outside. In all, there was a lot more space for drugs and this would enable us to stock the hundreds of millions of drugs which would be required for ECHO's expanding programme.

As the week passed the main thrust of the move was completed. The faithful staff battled on with the construction, alteration and repair programme, while the office staff struggled under extremely difficult conditions to keep the routine going. They were all very tired, but cheerful spirits and a sense of calling kept them in tune, and it was so evident that God gave the extra ability to cope in an obviously difficult situation. He is always at hand to give that superhuman strength when it is genuinely needed, and the staff were very conscious of His enabling at this time.

It was, however, quite amazing how quickly life returned to normal and how soon the staff settled into their new quarters and routine. The following story illustrates the constant buzz of activity involved in the day-to-day activities of this busy little concern.

'He's gone again.' Eleanor viewed the empty office, so often vacated by its active occupant. She made a beeline for the drug storage department, being pretty certain that she would find him there, somewhere between the boxes.

'Doctor, where are you?' she called, her voice lost in the mountainous piles of boxes and cartons.

'He must be somewhere amongst this lot,' she thought.

Suddenly, a flash of white identified the Doctor's coat, as he vanished round a large stack of iron tablets and, by the time she had reached those, he was skirting the aspirin shelf. It was not until he reached the multi-vitamins that she caught up with him.

'Doctor, can I have your attention for one moment, please?' she pleaded.

'Certainly,' replied James, in his usual, unruffled manner.

This game of hide and seek was quite common. James always liked to keep a strict eye on the drug stocks and the day-to-day activity in those days, often joining the warehouse team in the selecting, checking and packing of orders from the piles of boxes and array of metal shelves.

Just as they were getting down to the matter she wanted to discuss with him, the tannoy blared across the warehouse.

'John, can you go to the unloading bay, please? Thank you.'

James pricked up his ears.

'I wonder what has arrived,' he said. 'Hang on a minute, Eleanor. I must go and see.' And with that he was off, leaving his poor secretary in mid-sentence as he hurriedly made his way towards the loading bay.

Eleanor returned to her office, convinced that his 'minute' would allow her to have a coffee and do half a dozen more letters before it was up. In any case, she would probably have to put forward her own solution on this matter, or it would just have to rejoin the ever growing file of things 'to be attended to'. But at least she had succeeded in tracking him down on this occasion, and that in itself was a major victory.

Back at the unloading bay, John Kingsnorth was already heaving up the roller doors as a five-ton lorry vibrated in the forecourt.

'What's coming in?' asked James, as he bustled into view.

'The Dapsone consignment has arrived at last,' replied John.

We had been waiting for some time for this particular consignment; 15 million Dapsone tablets for treating leprosy patients. There were several outstanding orders awaiting despatch, as we had underestimated the tremendous demand that was now pressing upon us from every part of the leprosy-suffering world, and our earlier stocks had been exhausted. Our annual requirement of this drug alone now approached 150 million, compared to our first order for 1 million, made with much faith and anticipation just two years previously. There has been a tremendous advance in the use of this drug. Now, further supplies had come to complete new orders as they arrived, and we knew that there would be many more millions needed before the year was out.

Almost before John had finished rolling back the doors, the lorry revved up and backed slowly to the place appointed within the precincts of the warehouse. As the lorry shuddered to a halt, people appeared from every direction, as though obeying some mysterious signal. They all converged on the vehicle and in no time at all the back of the lorry was opened up to reveal its precious cargo.

It was a principle amongst the staff that when there was an urgent need in the unloading or packing department, all possible members, despite their normal tasks, leave the routine for a brief spell to deal with the emergency situation. Here was just such a situation, needing all available hands to get these Dapsone drugs moved toward their ultimate destination to treat one of the world's most dreaded diseases.

As the gathering collection of staff hovered round the intruding lorry, the chatter and clatter increased. Trolleys and fork-lifts trucks added to the drama, and the whole scene took on the appearance of a swarm of agitated wasps about to zoom into action.

'We've been waiting weeks for this order,' said James joyfully to the driver. 'Most of this Dapsone consignment will be flown out to India within the next few days, I hope. They've been waiting even longer.'

'Not my fault, Guv,' replied the driver. 'Called me out yesterday afternoon, they did; said it was urgent.' He leant up against the side of the lorry, stretched and yawned. 'Been travelling all through the night, I 'ave, Guv. Stopped for a kip along the way; bloomin' cold kip it was too ... Got 'ere as fast as I could...' He straightened up to his full lanky height and looked down on James with beady eyes.

'What's it do, this Dapsone stuff, Guv?'

'Oh, it's used to treat leprosy; one of the world's most dreaded diseases. There's enough here to treat 50,000 cases. They'll be thrilled to get it. Thanks a lot for your help.'

'Leprosy, what's leprosy, Guv?' asked the puzzled driver, lifting his cap and unobtrusively scratching his dishevelled hair.

As James placidly revealed the intricate details of the disease, the poor driver became more and more hypnotised; his jaw dropping and his eyes popped out of his head like organ stops.

'Cor ..., Guv, never 'eard of that before.'

His face took on an air of concentrated anxiety. 'Them poor blighters,' he gasped. 'Worth drivin' all night to 'elp 'em, ain't it, Guv?'

And with that, he staggered back to his cab. So the swarm began, as box after box was lifted and stacked and moved until the lorry was empty. Ninety boxes in all were unloaded, all added to the miscellany of boxes and crates of every size already scattered about the warehouse.

'Fourteen million eight hundred thousand ..., fourteen million nine hundred thousand ..., fifteen million,' exclaimed John, as he made the final checks, clamped his note pad and pen together and looked up with a smile.

'That's the lot.'

Fifteen million Dapsone tablets sounds a lot, but those would only be for a few orders, so great was the demand. Ten million would need to be reserved and urgently packed for a regular three-monthly consignment for the Leprosy Mission Hospital at Purulia in India, for distribution to hospitals and clinics specialising in the treatment of leprosy. The remainder would soon be despatched by air or sea freight to hospitals and clinics around the world, to join in the fight against one of the world's oldest and still, indeed, most dreaded diseases.

More and more missionary hospitals and relief programmes overseas were now relying on ECHO supplying their needs. With the cost of the move and the problems of settling into a much larger building, we only accepted a modest budget of £550,000 for our drug programme in 1979. It was evident that, with the increased staff and space, ECHO would achieve far more in the service of hundreds of missions and organisations now turning to ECHO for their supplies.

In faith, much larger orders had to be placed with manufacturers, vials of 2.5 million doses of Penicillin worth £37,500, and 150 million Leprosy drugs worth nearly £200,000. 'Cheaper by the million' had become ECHO's contribution to a vast world need that the organisation was being called to meet in the name of Christ.

Excellent relationships were being built up with many of the major pharmaceutical companies, and ECHO was able to obtain low contract prices enabling missionary doctors and nurses to get their drugs at some of the lowest prices available in the world. How God had honoured the decision of the ECHO Council of Management in 1975 to go forward on the pharmaceutical side of the work, thus enabling missions to reduce further the cost of modern medical work, and release hard-pressed missionary funds for other aspects of the churches' work.

Many amusing and thrilling incidents have taken place as ECHO has developed the new drug programme. One day, the Managing Director of the international company producing all the world's supply of raw material to produce Dapsone tablets arrived at ECHO (about 50 tons of this raw material are produced annually by the company).

'May I introduce myself, Doctor. I represent the manufacturing company... producing the raw material for Dapsone.'

'Oh yes,' said James politely. 'Do come into my office. I'm very pleased to meet you.'

'I've got a query concerning Dapsone orders and I wondered if you could help me?'

'I'll do my best; what's the problem?'

'Well, late last year, when we had our usual supply of about two tons of raw material on hand in the United Kingdom, we started to get unprecedented demands from three of the major generic tablet manufacturers in the U.K.'

'Oh yes,' exclaimed James, pricking up his ears in anticipation of what was coming.

'We couldn't keep pace with the U.K.'s needs, so enquired where it was all going. We were told that the tablets were all being produced for ECHO! One ton, you know, makes about 10 million leprosy drugs and we started to get demands for five tons and more. That's enough for 50 million tablets. We just couldn't understand what had suddenly happened to world leprosy demands! We thought it was time we met this ECHO organisation, so here I am.'

After a tour of the new headquarters, the company's representative was amazed at what he saw. He realised now that ECHO must be their principal customer, using, through its manufacturers, 25 tons of Dapsone raw material annually - 50% of the world's production. He was amazed to see orders like 10 million Dapsone tablets and another of 22.5 million Dapsone tablets piling up in the export crates in our warehouse.

Once a little organisation working in faith in a small warehouse by the London Docks in 1966, now one of the world's major supply agencies for the treatment of leprosy; how greatly the Lord had honoured and blessed us!

The company representative left ECHO with the amazing promise to see that ECHO got every assistance in the obtaining of enough Dapsone raw material through its manufacturers to meet world need. With the low prices resulting from such enormous bulk purchases, together with our non-profit-making policy, poorer nations would now be able to obtain the drug they needed at greatly reduced prices, to enable far greater numbers of Leprosy sufferers to be treated.

At this time a modern pharmaceutical factory in Malta, set up with overseas aid money from a Dutch development grant, offered ECHO the major part of their total production facilities of 500 million tablets, enabling ECHO to control its own pharmaceutical production needs from one of the world's first non-commercial pharmaceutical factories committed to the needs of the Third World. In 1980 we both flew out to Malta to visit the new ECHO pharmaceutical production programme in action. The work had grown tremendously during the year since production had begun, with over £1 million worth of tablets (500 million tablets) being produced to very high British Pharmaceutical Standards for the Third World. The factory now extended its premises as ECHO's needs increased. Some of the drugs produced in Malta were shipped or flown direct to their destinations and others were collected by European airlifts scheduled for specific emergency situations in Africa and Asia. These operations enabled us to cut costs even more.

World emergencies continued to place enormous pressures on our resources, as Cambodia, the Eritrean refugee problem in Somalia, the East African emergency, the Algerian earthquake and many other tragic situations overseas called on Christian organisations and people in the Western World for help. During one 48-hour period, 297 crates of medical supplies for Uganda to the value of £90,000 were packed and flown out for a Dutch Christian organisation. Three separate consignments, each weighing 40 tons, were packed for refugee camps in Somalia, where three-quarters of a million refugees were in desperate need of medical supplies and help. Each consignment left Ewell in 40-foot long box trailers overland and across the Channel to Bremen in Germany, to be flown out by the West German Air Force as part of an increasing international co-operation in medical aid work.

These projects all happened within a year of the move to Ewell, proving without doubt that the move to bigger premises had been essential if we were to be involved in world disasters to this extent, and to carry on our original purpose of supplying mission hospitals and medical concerns with their daily needs.

Also at this time, a further new development for ECHO was the creation of a European Emergency Stocks Committee formed of Christian organisations in Europe to co-ordinate the Christian Church's response to world need, and to speed up the supply of emergency stocks to disaster and refugee areas. ECHO was asked to join the supply side of the work, and this offered tremendous opportunities but, at the same time, created giant problems of supply and logistics worldwide. Several visits were made to European countries to co-ordinate this programme.

More and more requests came in to ECHO for help in the possible supply of vaccines and, as a result of extensive investigations and close co-operation with the World Health Organisation in Geneva, much help was arranged for medical missionaries involved in Primary Health Care programmes. These life-giving vaccines helped to halt the appalling toll of some five million little children under the age of five who were dying annually in the Third World from easily preventable diseases: measles, polio, tetanus, tuberculosis, diphtheria and whooping cough. ECHO developed its own 'cold chain' equipment, i.e. a special insulated bulk vaccine transit container, which just needed to be plugged into a car battery in transit to keep the precious vaccines at the right temperature.

One of the major projects that was started at Ewell was the formation of the Appropriate Technology Programme. This meant concentration on the design and production of simple medical equipment appropriate to the technology of the developing world. The best technology to make available to developing countries is the level of technology they can use to greatest advantage. It is totally unhelpful to send the very latest electronic diagnostic equipment somewhere without basic services of technicians trained to operate and maintain it. A computerised transistorised whole body x-ray scanner, for example, may be just what a London hospital needs, but what good is that if the overseas hospital has no electricity supply, or perhaps not even a decent table upon which to carry out surgery!

The equipment needed in the field might appear rather basic for the sophisticated idea of developed countries, but it is eminently suited for these areas.

Thus ECHO looked into the possibility of establishing a range of high-quality, low-priced, basic equipment items for mission hospitals. For instance, a simple operating table priced commercially at £1,500 would be manufactured for ECHO for £250. This operating table, made by a long-established equipment manufacturer to a simple design in light alloy, would incorporate many of the features of the heavy hydraulic operating table costing ten times as much. Ancillary equipment, too, was brought into consideration, such as a fixed operating stool, simplified Mayo table, a sterilizer for variable heating sources and an operating spotlight adapted to ECHO's design, small, portable and run from mains electricity, but with built-in capacity for easy conversion to use power from a car battery in the event of a mains failure. This latter item would also utilise car headlight bulbs, which are available in most countries of the world.

By 1981 some 20 different appropriate technology items were designed in this way. Thus, vast savings were created for hard-pressed medical missionary budgets, and investigations into the possibility of adding to the range of appropriate technology items continued.

17 : Now thank we all our God

With all these new developments, it was becoming obvious that even the Ewell premises were too small for the efficient running of the growing organisation. We really did need extra space for increased mechanisation and throughput of orders. By January 1982 this had become an increasing problem. Demands for supplies for mission and charity hospitals and a constant call for disaster and medical relief projects, were posing almost insurmountable problems for the staff. As jumbo-sized lorries, bringing in supplies, mixed with lorries carrying out packed consignments to airports and docks, it became apparent that urgent steps would soon need to be taken to ease the situation.

For some time also, we had been aware of the need to provide technical support for the increasing range of equipment now being provided by the organisation. There was a need to have spare parts available to maintain equipment on the field, and to be able to give comprehensive technical advice on all types of medical equipment. Also, we needed to enlarge and improve the range of high-quality reconditioned equipment available, at low cost, to the overseas mission and charity hospitals we served. There was no ending to what could be done if we had a specific department to deal with all this and other areas of technical service to the medical missionary, but there was certainly no room for this at Ewell.

Then, quite unexpectedly, our ancillary stores, a large vacant church hall in Sutton, had to be given up due to site development; thus the problem of accommodation and storage space was acutely exacerbated. At the same time, we had been challenged to open our own medical engineering division, which would need considerable extra space for the technical renovation of equipment, and for a complex spare parts and back-up maintenance service for our equipment in the field and other potential developments when the new service got under way.

Many times in the history of ECHO we have been driven to look to God for an answer to similar needs and, once more, our faith was rewarded. Concurrent with the need to vacate our Sutton stores, excellent new premises became available nearby at Chessington, with almost 10,000 square feet of extra space, which gave excellent temporary facilities for the setting up of the new Technical Department, and to give us the additional storage space we now required. So, yet another vision for the development and advancement of ECHO's services became a reality. A highly trained medical technician was engaged to head up this new department and further technical staff joined the project. Within weeks of its formation, the new department became functional, and it was now possible to extend the range of renovated medical equipment items, because of the engineering skills now available.

Although 'Chessington' gave a temporary breathing space to the organisation to enable its rapid development to continue, if ECHO was to continue expanding to serve a very needy world, then it was urgently necessary to get the whole ECHO operation under one roof as soon as possible. The situation at Ewell pointed in every way to a further move to much larger premises, absolutely essential if we were going to be in the position to respond to world disasters swiftly, and to hold the stocks to enable us to do so.

Then another bombshell dropped on the organisation. The Local Authority informed us that they would definitely require the site at Ewell at the termination of our lease in September 1984, and that we would not be able to renew it. So, once again, 'all things', including the termination of the lease, seemed to be 'working together for good' for ECHO and those we were serving. During the following months, an extensive 'search programme' was undertaken by ECHO's Administrative and Medical Directors. Many buildings were inspected and rejected as unsuitable, but finally an excellent modern building was found at Ullswater Crescent, Coulsdon, Surrey. Being close to Motorway connections to Gatwick and Heathrow Airports, and on a direct line from London mainline stations, the situation and the building seemed ideal in every way. There was only one snag! The building was on the market at just over £1 million. Surely, ECHO's faith was being stretched this time! As the building was so ideal, a giant step of faith was taken by the ECHO Council of Management. As the current owners wished to have up to 12 months to relocate, we signed the contract for the reduced sum of £840,000, giving ECHO time to raise this gigantic sum and the owners time to relocate. The Sudan Interior Mission, one of our Member Missions, who were also searching for a new modern headquarters, joined with ECHO and took one floor of offices in the new building for their British headquarters, and we decided the building should be known as The Joint Mission Centre.

But, with a total expenditure of £905,000 to face, due to extra building work that would need to be carried out before the building could be equipped for the work of ECHO, much careful and prayerful financial planning had to take place. In the autumn of 1983, the then Chairman of ECHO, Mr. David Clement CBE, challenged the wide ECHO membership with the immensity of the tasks facing ECHO and for the organisation to take this major step forward in acquiring adequate premises to fulfil these tasks in the service of our members. As the first phase of a special new Warehouse and Development Appeal Fund was to be set up, Mr. Clement shared with our members this enormous step forward we were taking. We were humbled by the overwhelming generous response, in grants, interest-free and low-interest bearing loans that we received, reassuring us of the support and confidence of our wide membership in the work we were carrying out on their behalf.

In February, 1984, Lord Porrit, the President of ECHO, launched the second stage of the ECHO development and Warehouse Appeal for the sum of £500,000 with the support of many prominent people in public life. Again, there was a widespread and generous response from many grant making Trusts and Foundations, City Livery Companies, Industry and the Banking world, as well as many private individuals. Many interested friends joined us in this biggest challenge that the organisation had ever faced. By their gifts and by many fund raising efforts, such as coffee mornings, stamp collecting and sales, choir concerts, bring and buy sales, Webb Ivory sales, sponsored walks and other activities, gifts began to pour into the organisation. We acknowledged too, in thankfulness to God, the gifts received from some people who auctioned some of their possessions through the Wallington Missionary Mart auctions, and channelled the gifts to this big development facing ECHO. An extensive programme of public meetings was organised around the country for the showing of the ECHO film presentation, and this, together with the sale of greetings and Christmas cards and books, all contributed to the fund. ECHO's former smaller Sutton headquarters, which had been leased for several years, was also sold to augment the fund.

The task of moving ECHO from its buildings at Ewell and Chessington to South Coulsdon was a mammoth one. With hundreds of tons of stores to move, the staff undertook much of the move themselves, reducing the cheapest commercial removal estimate of £27,000 to under £5,000 by hiring a fleet of lorries and using a great deal of elbow grease! Considerable building and decorating work had to be undertaken to fit the building for its new tasks. For instance, to maximise storage and display space, the mezzanine flooring was extended, and special steelwork erected to house the heavy goods lift, which was transferred in its entirety from Ewell. It was also necessary to install heating throughout the building and do other essential building work demanded by the authorities for the new purpose for which the building was to be used. In addition, very considerable fire regulations work had to be undertaken, in view of ECHO's large staff that was to move into the building.

Alongside all the building and decorating work that was going on around the staff, unprecedented demands for ECHO's services were continuing to be received, not only for the supply of 2,000 missionary hospitals and medical relief programmes, but also with calls from many national and international charities for relief supplies. Even before ECHO had completed the transaction of moving from one building to the next, desperate calls came from the U.K. and international aid organisations to help in the tragic situation in Ethiopia and the Sudan, with food and emergency medical supplies for hundreds and thousands of starving and suffering people. Indeed, an additional £1 million worth of supplies were despatched in the first quarter of 1985, despite the extensive building work going on all around us. Nevertheless, by 9th May, 1985, everything was in order and ready for the official opening of the Headquarters. So much had happened in the preceding year, and it seemed a miracle, as indeed it was, that ECHO now had its own permanent new home from which to face the challenge of the future. On the morning of the 9th May, representatives of the wide ECHO membership gathered for the Annual General Meeting, as the work of 1984 was reported on, and all our plans for future development shared.

In the afternoon, 500 guests from many parts of the United Kingdom and Europe arrived and gathered in the large packing area of the warehouse that had been stripped the evening before of all its packing benches, in readiness for the event.

A Service of Dedication was conducted by the former Archbishop of Canterbury, The Rt. Hon. The Lord Coggan. Mr. Clement, the retiring Chairman of ECHO, welcomed guests and spoke briefly of the enormous strides of development that the organisation had made in the service of a very needy world. Lord Coggan spoke of his first-hand contact with ECHO's work in missionary hospitals, and consecrated the building to the Glory of God and its worldwide service. During the service, two great hymns of praise rang out through the building and re-echoed round every corner and passage, in praise to our God who had made all this possible and had brought us to this crowning day. 'Now thank we all our God...' and 'Praise

Opening of the new Coulsdon Joint Mission Centre by Lord Coggan in 1985

my soul the King of Heaven...' We really meant every word we sang; our hearts were full of praise as we realised how much God had blessed the organisation through the years, and would continue to do so in the tasks of the future.

Following the Service of Dedication, guests gathered in the large forecourt of the building, Mr. J. Fforde, elected that day as the new Chairman of ECHO, introduced the Rt. Hon. The Lord Porritt, who had so ably served the organisation as its first Chairman and then became its President through the 19 years of its history. Lord Porritt spoke of the development of ECHO from its small beginnings, equating the size of its previous headquarters with the increasing tasks the organisation had been able to take on around the world. He also welcomed the Sudan Interior Mission, who were to use part of the building as their British Headquarters. He then cut the symbolic tape and, as the curtain fell away, the name of the new Headquarters was revealed as 'The Joint Mission Centre'. To God be the Glory!

After Lord Porritt had declared the building open, assembled visitors split into groups led by senior members of ECHO's staff for conducted tours of the building. They saw the many facets of ECHO's work and the warehouse packed with supplies awaiting shipment by air and sea to many different Third World destinations, including supplies continuously desperately needed for the ongoing emergency in the African famine areas.

The Joint Mission Centre warehouse and offices, Coulsdon

So the day drew to a close as our guests and staff travelled home with the words of the hymn sung earlier in the afternoon ringing in their ears:

'Now thank we all our God
With hearts and hands and voices
Who wondrous things hath done
In whom His world rejoices.'

18 : World emergencies

ECHO represented the first organised and co-ordinated attempt in the United Kingdom to deal with the acquisition, servicing and transport of equipment to mission hospitals and medical relief work overseas. It was, therefore, well placed to supply very large stocks of surgical and medical equipment to meet crisis calls from the major United Kingdom charities and other Christian bodies for national disasters. Oxfam, Christian Aid, Save the Children Fund, War on Want, Tear Fund, The Catholic Fund for Overseas Development and the British Red Cross, all came to ECHO for practical help. Missions and charities from many other countries in the Western world were also now seeking help from ECHO, so that at least 50% of the material supplied was being requested through non-British agencies.

One of the first major calls on ECHO's resources was the crisis in Biafra some years ago. At the request of Oxfam and Save the Children Fund, 14 enormous crates of medical supplies and equipment were prepared for 7 medical teams and flown out to Biafra within 48 hours of the cry for help from thousands of starving children in that country. The value of the goods sent amounted to £20,000. We charged Oxfam our own costs amounting to £600.

Since then, supplies have been rushed to many disaster areas. In 1974, for instance, urgently needed equipment and drugs were sent to Bangladesh to help the vast scale of suffering in refugee camps, due to widespread flooding. On another occasion, thoracic surgical equipment and other supplies were requested for victims of an earthquake in Peru. These were supplied and delivered to the Peruvian Embassy in London within 24 hours of the initial request. On another occasion there was a volcanic eruption in the Comoros Islands; a call from the British Red Cross came for a £5,000 order of emergency supplies to be delivered by 4 o'clock the same afternoon at their London headquarters for a flight out that evening. The deadline was met. Another emergency involved an airlift organised through the Norwegian Church Relief and Swedish Church Relief, to help in appalling refugee problems caused by the Eritrean conflict.

A few days previously, at 2.00 p.m. one afternoon a telex message was received in London from the United Nations High Commissioner in Khartoum; an emergency on the Eritrea border necessitated a team of paediatric doctors to save the lives of thousands of starving refugee children. They needed thousands of infant gastric feeding tubes, butterfly scalp vein cannulae and sterilising equipment. The call came to the Institute of Child Health who passed it on to ECHO. By 5 p.m. the same day the order was ready and a commercial company working in Khartoum air-freighted the supplies. ECHO was able to supply all the requirements.

Another example occurred when Oxfam was requested by the Somaliland Government to help in supplying a complete Field Hospital to cater for an urgent refugee problem. Oxfam could supply the tents for the hospital - could we supply everything else, from a very long list of equipment laid down for a Field Hospital by the British Ministry of Defence? The list included over a hundred different drugs. We promised delivery of everything in 21 days, and the whole Field Hospital was packed and ready for shipment in this time. ECHO was also able to prune Oxfam's estimate of between £12,000 and £14,000 to £6,000.

On one occasion, an earthquake in Guatemala; on another occasion a call from Tear Fund to supply cots and equipment for 100 Vietnamese orphans being flown to Britain to stay at Keffolds, of the Ockenden Venture at Haslemere, Surrey. In 1982, the needs of the Polish people stirred the hearts and consciences of the Western world and almost every Christian and relief organisation we deal with responded and an amazing total of nearly 100 consignments were sent by ECHO to the value of £150,000 - food, medicine and medical equipment were trucked across Europe to bring relief to orphanages, children's hospitals, church communities, etc.

Thus, through the years, ECHO has been called into many other emergencies, too numerous to mention in the contents of this book.

One emergency at Coulsdon, however, deserves a mention here. On the afternoon of December 6th, 1984, Mrs. Victoria Wells, head of ECHO's Medical Equipment Department, noticed the telex machine rattling off a particularly long message. It was from the Overseas Development Administrators (O.D.A.) in London and was marked 'URGENT'.

Mrs. Wells (affectionately known as 'Vicky') picked up the message, gasped, then paused for a few moments to digest the magnitude of the request.

'Goodness,' she exclaimed to nobody in particular. 'Wherever are we going to get all this?' She hastened over to James' office in a flurry of excitement, waving the lengthy telex message as she came to an abrupt halt in front of his desk.

'Take a look at this,' she said, as she handed James the list.

'Oh! This must be in response to that terrible gas disaster for which we sent 10,000 packs of eye drugs with the British team of eye surgeons for the Royal Commonwealth Society for the Blind. I thought they would be on to us for supplies before long. Let's see what they want.'

Three days had already passed since a thick white cloud of gas had seeped out of a ruptured valve from an underground storage tank of a pesticide factory on the outskirts of the central Indian town of Bhopal. Fanned by a stiff breeze, the gas cloud swept across the neighbouring shanty town, along the railway track and across the railway station, contaminating the air over a 50 square kilometre area. With a night temperature around 13°C, the gas cloud hung low, hugging the ground and engulfing homes and huts across its path. Within 45 minutes the ruptured valve of the gas tank had been sealed, but it was 45 minutes too late. The escaping gas was the highly toxic methyl isocyanate, widely used in the manufacture of pesticides, but lethal if inhaled by humans or any other living creatures.

Many thousands of citizens had woken up coughing and fighting for breath; scores died in their beds within minutes. Tens of thousands were rushed to hospital and makeshift medical centres; tens of thousands more had fled the city but, having already inhaled the gas, were forced to seek medical help. Over 2,500 people, mostly children and elderly people, died. Fifty thousand people suffered temporary blindness and severe eye irritation, and some 150,000 more suffered from other forms of lung injury due to the poison.

Within hours, news of this human tragedy (one of the greatest industrial accidents of all time) had hit the news coverage of the whole world and, as the world looked on in horror, hundreds of Indian doctors and voluntary workers, assisted by specialist teams, rushed from other countries to begin a gigantic relief task.

'It's quite a list, isn't it?' exclaimed James, as he glanced over the many requests: 50 laryngoscopes, 300 oxygen flow meters, 100 oxygen valves, 100 regulating valves, 200 tracheotomy tubes, 200 endotracheal tubes, 25 tracheal tubes, 150 sets of airways, 100 sets of connections, 5,000 pollymasks, 400 resuscitation bags, 74 paediatric laryngoscope sets, 200 endohocheal forceps, 20 ventilators, 2,000 angio catheters, 100 sets of monitoring equipment, 125 electrical section apparatus, 18 cardiac machines and a long list of other equipment.

'Phew!' James relaxed back in his swivel chair, resting his head in his hand. 'Where do you begin, Vicky? You'll have to contact every manufacturer in the U.K. We must move fast, no time to waste; enough has been wasted already, but you'll manage,' he said as optimistically as ever.

As was his custom on these occasions, James contacted Bill Davies, his colleague, immediately and told him the news.

'But we're in the middle of a rushed job for CAFOD and that Oxfam order hasn't been dealt with yet, and in any case, where in the world do we find all that in a hurry?'

Bill was in the middle of end-of-year statistics and to have this news thrust at him at the end of a busy day didn't help the situation.

James stretched his full 5 ft. 6 ins. 'Leave it to Vicky; she'll get cracking and see what can be done. Difficult jobs take a little time to organise; impossible ones take a little longer!' And with that he disappeared to co-ordinate with Vicky, who had already alerted her work team.

Rapid phone calls to the O.D.A. confirmed that the plane carrying these supplies hoped to leave by early the next week, leaving just one working day to obtain all these supplies before British factories and suppliers closed down for the weekend. This meant calling in a quarter of a million pounds' worth of highly specialised medical equipment in 24 hours. So began one of the most 'impossible' tasks of ECHO's history.

The next day, supplies began to roll in to Coulsdon from all over the U.K. Some companies even stripped their showrooms in order to make up the vast quantities needed to complete the order. As soon as supplies started to arrive, ECHO staff in every department got to work.

Colin with his team of willing packers stripped the packing area ready for action, and as fast as Michael made up boxes, willing hands packed away the needed items. Each box had to be marked with its destination, steel banded for protection and weighed for the airway documents; a huge pile of finished boxes soon began to mount.

But packing the boxes was just one of many vital tasks; documents had to be prepared, airway bills organised and all arrangements made by Mrs. Ivy Wileman, the hard-working head of our Shipping Department. These documents would ensure that the goods were delivered to the airport on time for the scheduled cargo flight to India.

'Dr. Burton! Dr. Burton!' the tannoy blared out over this seething hive of activity. 'Visitors are waiting for you in the reception.'

'Now that's all we need,' James muttered as he literally trotted in and out of the organised chaos of boxes, trolleys and workers in answer to the call.

Visitors are always welcome to come and see what is going on at the heart of things; convenient or not, they cannot be ignored and this was no exception. Often they are missionaries who come to choose equipment or drugs to take back to their medical centres, or sometimes they are from supporting churches or merely interested individuals.

On this occasion these were viewing visitors and, as if nothing in particular was happening, James conducted them round the various departments as if he was a tour guide in the Tower of London. Of course, when they reached the packing department, the scene before them changed abruptly and resembled something like Covent Garden market at dawn, except here were valuable pieces of equipment being tossed around instead of carrots and cauliflowers!

'My! You are busy!' exclaimed the amazed visitors.

'Just one of our emergencies,' retorted James, as if this sort of thing was a continual process of the daily routine. He did, however, explain what it was all about.

'It's here,' shouted a voice from a distance, and low rumbles indicated the arrival of the giant lorry sent to convey the boxes to the airport.

'Oh! Over this way, please,' said James politely to his visitors, as the forklift came rumbling through the crates and boxes with a great load, nearly catching one of the visitors a broadsider, as it hastened on its way towards the loading bay.

'I think we had better move back to the office,' James suggested diplomatically and, without further ado, he led his bewildered visitors away from the battle front to the more peaceful environs of his office where, by now, Sylvia had added height to the already untouched mail on his desk.

So, the bustle of activity continued until 183 large boxes of hospital equipment left on schedule. This was to be followed the next day by a further 92 boxes to fill a second plane.

The exhausted staff, who had so faithfully worked so hard, breathed a sigh of relief, but went home rejoicing after the two-day marathon; a task well done and the impossible made possible by the team work and devotion of a small dedicated staff, just doing their job to the best of their ability.

I am sure readers would like to read extracts of the letter sent to Mr. William Davies, the Administrative Director of ECHO, from the grateful British Overseas Development Administration.

Dear Mr. Davies,

I am writing to you about the medical equipment you obtained and air-freighted to India, on our behalf, following the horrendous leak of lethal gas in Bhopal... I first contacted ECHO on December 6th to enquire about the availability of a whole range of equipment... all of which was vitally needed. The response I received, the advice and assistance that I was given was immediate. The result was, that only six days later some two tonnes of equipment had been obtained, packed and air-freighted to Delhi and the balance following the next day.

I am very conscious of the fact that this was done at a time when you were all under great pressure supplying the needs of the many agencies operating in Ethiopia and elsewhere and when you were still suffering the upheavals of having moved into new premises. May I therefore ask you to pass on my sincere thanks to all who contributed to this really swift and professional response. I can assure you that their efforts, for which there is genuine appreciation and admiration both in Bhopal and Delhi, were not in vain. I am advised that all the equipment arrived in good condition in Bhopal on December 13th and had all been distributed to and put to use by the various medical institutions of Bhopal by the 16th...

Again my sincere thanks to you all.

R. B. Emery
Overseas Development Administration

Another natural disaster to mention here is the Nevado de Ruiz volcano, in North West Columbia, which erupted on November 14th, 1985. More than 20,000 people lost their lives; many drowned in their sleep. The volcano's melted ice cap sent torrents of mud into a 70 square mile area, and the town of Armero was completely engulfed in the mud stream.

The first hint of real trouble came just five minutes after three o'clock in the afternoon. The ground began to shake. Ten minutes after the first tremor, a peasant on the northern slope of the volcano, a few kilometres from the summit, saw Mount Ruiz erupt, emitting a long column of black ash high up into the sky. There was a deep rumbling noise from the bowels of the mountain. About half an hour later, evacuation from this area was advised. There was very limited response to the call to evacuate and, as night fell, around 7 p.m., a heavy rainstorm struck the small town and loud thunder claps drowned the rumbling noises from the volcano. After this there were continuous tremors and two strong explosions. These increased, followed by a 45 minute rain of water, hot pumice blocks, ash and soil. This mixture sped down the mountainside, gaining speeds reaching 30 miles per hour, as it descended along the Azugrado River channel and Lagunilla River. The mud flow arrived with such force that it collapsed a natural dam on the Lagunilla and swept away the town of Armero, located about 45 kilometres from the crater. It caused another river to overflow, carrying away houses and a bridge on the main road to the Colombian capital, Bogota.

On the western side of the mountain, another mudslide descended upon a coffee growing area, destroying some 400 houses and killing over 1,000 people. 'The avalanche of mud rolled into the town with a moaning sound, like some kind of monster,' reported one survivor. 'Houses below us started cracking under the avalanche of the river mud. It seemed like the end of the world.' There were few survivors. Those who did live recounted almost unbelievable tales of people frantically trying to outrace the mud flow. 'Some were crying to God,' said one policeman. 'They were running helplessly in circles; it was terrible.' Some residents fled on foot; others locked themselves in vehicles, hoping to ride out the wave. Few succeeded.

The world was first informed when Armero's mayor was talking via home radio to a fellow operator in a nearby town. He was describing the eruption when he suddenly cried, 'Wait a minute. I think the town is getting flooded.' Those were his last words. At about the same time, a Red Cross official in Armero was discussing over the radio the need to launch a full scale volcano alert. The Armero official abruptly yelled, 'The water is coming! The water is coming!' whereupon the radio went dead.

Despite generous and rapid offers of aid, on-site relief efforts were slowed down by difficult weather conditions, mudslides and showers of ash, hindering supply deliveries and the arrival of helicopters and rescue teams. It was not until the 15th that the large helicopters could get through. Meanwhile, nine small helicopters worked unceasingly, rescuing a handful of people each trip. Working against time, rescuers improvised caring for survivors as best as they could. Survivors, some buried to the neck, were dragged away from the drying mud on tyres used as makeshift sleds. Hospitals were filled all too soon, and rescue operators lamented the lack of medicine and clothing. Still, amidst the confusion and horror, heroes were born and miracles were made.

The first call of this disaster came to ECHO on November 18th from Oxfam for a very long list of medical equipment, drugs and supplies needed for the relief teams - 17 kinds of drugs, rehydration salts and water purifying tablets. Also, 87 different types of equipment - plaster shears, surgical instruments, dressings, intravenous sets, etc. This was swiftly followed by requests from the British Red Cross Society, the British Overseas Development Administration and the Friends of Colombia for social aid.

Amongst the many gifts that came into ECHO for help and to be spent on supplies for treatment of the injured, was a grant from the Trustees of the Cloth-workers Foundations of the City of London. They telephoned ECHO to ask if £1,000 could be used, and we were able to tell them that their grant had miraculously met a very real need. Supplies for the British Red Cross relief operation had exactly overspent their allocation of aid funds by £1,000! How wonderfully God supplies the needs of his people in these miraculous ways. It is so necessary for us to have faith that sincerely believes in a God of the impossible.

Many of us were watching the horrific pictures on the television that evening and some of us noticed in particular the urgent request from Colombia for x-ray film and supplies, as the surrounding hospitals had exhausted their supplies. The next day Mr. Davies telexed the British Embassy in Bogota to confirm this need. ECHO had the necessary goods in stock and immediately decided to strip £1,000 worth of film and equipment from the shelves as a donation to meet it. The whole consignment weighed just under 2 tons. Twenty-four hours later this x-ray equipment was in Bogota, being distributed to the hospitals desperately needing it, in particular to cope with multiple arm and leg fractures.

It was a real encouragement to receive the following letter from the British Embassy, Bogota, a while later:

'Your gift of x-ray film and developer arrived by Air France in the early hours of 24th November, and was immediately handed over (with the ODA/Red Cross consignment) to the National Hospital Fund of the Ministry of Health. This is the body co-ordinating the supply of emergency medical items to the various hospitals treating those injured in the Ruiz disaster.

The Fund representatives were most appreciative of your donation and anticipated that the x-ray material would be the most urgently used of any of the items in the consignment.

I should like to add my thanks and congratulate you on the speed with which you reacted.'

So, in between the day-to-day tasks of output to hundreds of mission hospitals, ECHO responds to calls from more and more Relief Organisations. Often they are presented with seemingly impossible tasks, and seldom does a week go by without urgent calls to ECHO for assistance in some crisis call to the Christian Church to help provide relief in the event of a disaster. But, from the variety of examples in this chapter, it is obvious that ECHO has proved time and again its adaptability in being able to fit into every kind of situation which involves the relief of suffering and showing concern for people in need.

Thus, ECHO became more and more involved in a cross section of world emergencies, and the challenge increases as the years go by.

....oOo....

19 : Famine relief

In 1985, a new chapter opened in ECHO's history. Whereas in the past ECHO has been asked to respond from time to time with supplies for world disasters, we now had calls from worldwide Christian relief organisations and world charities as never before, to supply their needs for worldwide disaster situations. Over 1 million kg (1,000 tonnes) of supplies left our warehouse for emergency and disaster relief in many nations during 1985. Naturally, the desperate conditions in the great drought and famine belt of Africa gave us our greatest challenge. The last great famine was in 1975, but in 1985 more than three times as many had died during the greatest famine in living memory.

Part of the cause of this tragic disaster stems back to colonial days when African countries were encouraged to grow single cash crops such as coffee, tea, cocoa and fruit for export; this meant that food production for local consumption was severely restricted. This situation still exists to a certain extent through multinational companies and large land owners. Vital foreign exchange can thus be made available through using every fertile area to be found for the growing of these cash crops; this had often meant that government help has been restricted to the 'export earners' rather than to small farmers, struggling to maintain crops for local consumption. Statistics show a dramatic fall in food production over the past decade.

Other causes involved were crises of a social and political nature, often with war situations as well. But the famine in 1985 which affected so many parts of Africa in this belt was basically due to a natural phenomenon of drought, complicated by human error. As a result, the sum of human misery was out of all proportion and many thousands of innocent people died in the wake of an overwhelming tragedy.

Drought in itself does not necessarily lead to a major emergency but the main cause goes back a long way. At one time forest covered this area and the land was fertile, but over the years deforestation has taken place at an alarming rate as wood has provided the only cooking fuel which the peasants could afford, and companies have cut vast areas of mahogany trees for furniture production. No major reforestation programmes have been undertaken and small farmers have not been encouraged to use crop or land rotation. Thus, productive land became desert at an alarming rate. The trees had held the soil together but then when the rains did come, there was nothing to prevent the top soil being washed away, making the land impossible to cultivate. Overgrazing has also led to depletion and deterioration of animal stocks.

Thus, where vegetation cover has been continually reduced over large areas, the resulting increase in dust levels and solar radiation reflection has tended to cause lower, unreliable rainfall by suppressing rain-cloud formation and retarding the normal progress of the summer monsoon systems. So, the result of all this was drought, causing farmers and nomads to sell off their assets, leave their homes and land and migrate to cities, the land being left to deteriorate further. If measures are not taken to keep people on the land with adequate development of land cultivation, then famine follows drought and this is precisely the situation that developed and spread across a wide belt of African countries at such a speed.

Famine means there is no food available for a large number of people and often whole villages are forced to leave their homes and grazing lands to become dependent on relief supplies. Famine is not a sudden phenomenon, but it speeds up the process of malnutrition, bringing people to the point of death through starvation.

This chapter mainly covers Ethiopia, but all the countries in the famine belt are now in a similar situation, and conditions are just as critical. For instance, in 1985 some 700,000 Ethiopians made the month-long trek to the desperately overcrowded refugee camps in Sudan. Another camp intended for 30,000 had to cope with 50,000 until new camps could be organised. In

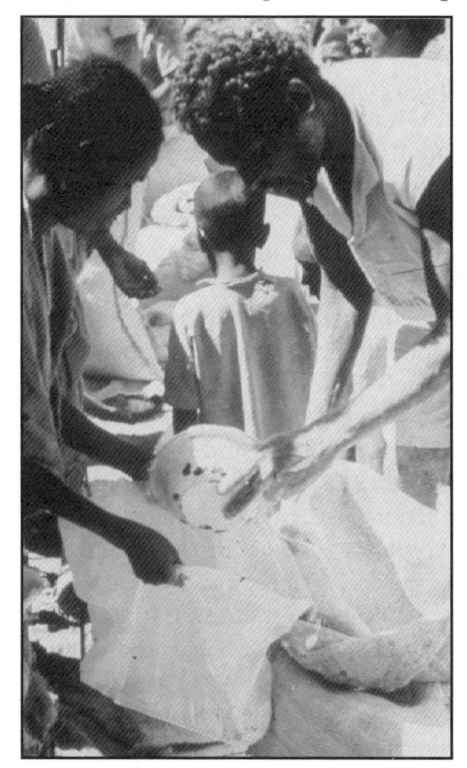

Famine relief in Ethiopia

Western Sudan, over 1 million Sudanese were afflicted by drought and thousands of refugees from Chad crossed into that country. In the Tigre highlands of Ethiopia, Oxfam introduced soil conservation measures designed to trap flood waters and spread them over agricultural areas in an effort to correct the worsening situation there.

By 1985, there was a race against time in the Sudan. Food was getting through to keep people alive and emergency feeding was being carried out in the villages, despite the appalling road conditions, but there was a desperate need to get out of emergency feeding into long-term development; billions of pounds would be needed over many years.

However, by 1986, more than 13,000 refugees who had fled into Sudan to escape famine and civil war in the north of Ethiopia, had returned home after dramatic improvements in health. At one camp the number of refugees dwindled from 20,000 to less than 7,000, and the Sudanese government decided to convert the camp into a permanent settlement for Eritrean refugees currently enduring desperate conditions in the desert. As a long-term project, they were encouraged to set up vegetable gardens and learn such skills as weaving, etc.

It was in 1982 that a warning of advancing conditions of the famine failed to attract sufficient response from western governments until the emergency actually struck. In 1984, the Disasters Emergency Committee succeeded in raising a record £9.25 million for famine relief, but even this failed to stimulate adequate government response.

Despite all this, it took Michael Buerk's report and harrowing pictures of thousands of famine victims on B.B.C. television in October 1984 to awaken the world to the scale of the tragedy, which neither the Ethiopians nor the major aid agencies involved had been able to effect. Thus, famine in Africa became the subject of press cuttings and television documentaries. Live Aid concerts and a host of other-Aid activities raised desperately needed finance for immediate and long-term help. The death toll rose and the number of countries affected began to multiply. The cameras revealed appalling sights; pathetic little children in emergency mortuaries, then a vast sea of sad-faced emaciated bodies, gazing into space; people for whom Christ gave His life; people without hope but nevertheless people. As Christians, we have been commanded to love one another. That doesn't mean just our best friends.

The world was finally shocked into action as hearts of believers and non-believers alike worldwide were touched and stirred. What began as an emotional response to visual stimulus was quickly translated into a public demand, right across the political spectrum for more substantial and effective government aid.

Thus, in November, 1985, ECHO tackled its biggest air charter to date for 'Mission Air Service', the relief wing of the Baptist World Alliance, which was paid for by churches from many nations, including the U.K.

A Boeing 747 jumbo cargo plane was chartered, and into its giant interior were packed 150 tonnes of life-giving relief supplies, including two trucks and thousands of blankets and baby vests. Two of our ECHO staff - Mrs. Ivy Wileman and Mrs. Anne Gwynn - accompanied the flight and their experiences are recorded in the following pages. They were taken by bus to the passenger terminal for immigration and customs, then to the plane, where the goods were being loaded. Anne reports: 'It was good to see the soya flour, oil and all the other things waiting to be forklifted into the nose of the plane... We were asked to get on board, and had to climb a ladder into the passenger cabin containing 15 seats and lots of leg room.' There was some consternation amongst Heathrow authorities, as ladies don't usually fly on cargo planes!!

Landing at Addis Airport the next morning, the big plane caused quite a stir, and many people came to look at it, never having seen a 'jumbo' of that sort before!

'We had the feeling of being thousands of miles from home and family,' says Ivy, 'and feeling very lonely.'

But after the plane was unloaded, Ivy and Anne were driven along the rough roads and were warmly welcomed by missionaries at the Southern Baptist Mission; all feelings of loneliness soon disappeared.

After a day to meet workers in Addis and the leader of the Christian Relief and Development Association, who co-ordinates all the relief supplies and their transportation in Ethiopia, they prepared for a helicopter trip to five of the feeding camps.

The paved road that leads north from Addis Ababa, leads to the drought areas, but it would take 8 hours to reach the first camp, whereas the same distance by helicopter would take just 6 minutes and carry some 3,500 lbs. of food.

'We set off at 9 a.m.,' writes Anne. 'The scenery was fantastic; little villages with mud huts in the compounds. All very neat and tidy. Then up 2,000 ft., making a total of 10,000 ft. above sea level. From then on it was like Grand Canyon after Grand Canyon, absolutely fantastic.'

Their first stop was at Camp Bete - a feeding station with a hospital, established by the R.R.C., but staffed by volunteer Canadians. The love that flowed out from doctors and nurses to those Ethiopian people who were sick and in desperate need, had a profound effect upon our two staff.

'It was marvellous to see the RAF doing their drops,' remarks Ivy. 'A tremendous feat of flying. They seemed to come so low that we wondered whether they would ever be able to gain height again.'

Ivy and Anne were thrilled to see lots of ECHO supplies and drugs in all the camps, proving that supplies were getting through. They found everything very primitive, and cleanliness at the health centre left much to be desired. In one small 'hospital theatre', the operating table consisted of two camp beds on top of each other and the sterilizer was plugged into a transformer on the ground.

'The people at the feeding camp were not allowed into the hospital compound,' writes Anne. 'But outside, they were very intrigued with us and took our hands; some spoke English and asked us our names and what was our country. They are very polite people, but their clothes were incredible, some just holes held together with bits of cloth.'

Let us examine some other conditions in the disaster area. For the people of Ethiopia, tomorrow is something they can barely imagine; their concern is for day-to-day survival, and they are thankful for any scrap of food they can come by.

At Debre Sina, 11,000 ft. up in the mountains, a huddled group of emaciated people sat exhausted by the wayside. They had walked from Karakore, some 125 miles away, having sold all their possessions in a desperate effort to buy food and remain alive. Entrance to a relief camp was denied them for some reason so they set out for Addis, hoping to find succour there. The likelihood was that they would never arrive; like hundreds before them, they would die en route.

Another family walked some 300 miles to reach Asmara; it took a month. As peasant farmers they had lost their livelihood when three rainless years scorched the earth and their cattle died. At Asmara they hoped for work but there was none, so they lived on the streets and depended on aid for their survival. When rations ran low, there was fear and panic, and then nothing.

Others did not reach the camps alive; on the rough roads and tracks a constant flow of people came into the camps. Many had abandoned homes and trekked for weeks, leaving the old and sick and weakest behind to die; others died by the wayside, and some were too sick to be helped when they did arrive.

Those who were fortunate enough to reach the camps joined the nightmare picture of tragedy which was repeated throughout the refugee camps; a vast area of hundreds upon hundreds of people in ragged clothes with possibly a scrap of cloth to provide some sort of shelter. Occasionally, a little stick fire provided some warmth during the cold nights, otherwise they just lay limply upon the bare ground; flies crawling over everything and everyone.

As rations were distributed, a long line formed, mothers and babies, wizened old men, children; all waited with resignation bordering on despair. The line inched forward as the rations of grain rapidly diminished; they moved away clutching their precious cargo, often grovelling in the dust to secure a few more grains that had dropped. A blind man formed part of the queue, led by his son. He came from Tigre province, where he supported his wife and four children by farming. When the rains stopped, they left in the hope of finding food elsewhere, and made the 120-mile journey on foot to the nearest camp. Another in the queue was a 20-year-old mother, who watched her two-year-old daughter playing in the dust. She had walked over 200 miles to reach the camp, leaving behind a smallholding of cows, sheep and vegetables. Her husband left her when the drought came and the animals died. The situation was repeated over and over; the story was the same.

The main problems over and above the malnutrition were dysentery, malaria and cholera. At the camp clinic it was a question of going around the compound outside the clinic, choosing those who could come in first for treatment. The choice was based upon whether it was too late for treatment or whether the quantity of medicine available was adequate.

All camps had the same story of hundreds of deaths daily. The poorest were the most vulnerable and the children virtual skeletons, so lifeless that one feared to disturb them in case they proved to be dead. Many of the children arriving at the camps were less than 80% of their correct weight. Some were in a sorry state and could not initially take solid food; they had to be fed by intravenous fluid - ECHO sent out thousands of scalp vein cannulae for this purpose - little babies would suck lethargically at their mother's empty breasts; it was all so pathetic. The children had the familiar symptoms of malnutrition: bloated stomachs and spindly legs. All this disappeared, however, as the children gained weight.

Malnourished children are much more vulnerable to disease caused through contaminated water; in one area a stream about 200 ft. down a mountainside was the only supply available, but this was contaminated and infested with Bilharzia. Ten to twenty litres of water per person per day was generally needed for drinking and cooking alone in the hot, dry climate; more for washing and for animals. That was an awful lot of water for the tens of thousands of refugees in each camp. The main task was to find adequate supplies of clean water - from rivers or wells, and protect these supplies from pollution by supplying pumping units, large storage tanks, pipes and taps. There was no quick or simple way to achieve that ideal.

Existing water had to be purified also to combat disease.

The main visit of Anne and Ivy was to the large Lemi feeding camp, which they reached by helicopter. They found the camp extremely busy, as emergency food to 200 families was being handed out.

They reported that the people formed a sitting queue all around the compound fence and then filed into the weighing and measuring room. The results were then recorded in a weight and height chart. The children's ears were painted with gentian violet so that they could not come back next day for more. The families then filed through the store and, depending on the weight of the children, they were given biscuits, milk, grain, oil and wheat, much of which was supplied by ECHO. These biscuits are special energy biscuits, created by Oxfam and sent out by the ton to the refugee camps. They have been produced as a supplementary food for use in emergencies, and they are intended to fill the gap which occurs in most disasters, until more suitable foods become available. They are similar to shortbread in texture and one packet of two biscuits will keep a child alive for 24 hours, each biscuit providing 125 calories. Even the empty containers are useful for carrying water.

Ivy and Anne spent much of their time at Lemi handing out blankets to each family and vests to each child, who were delighted with them. The relief flight had carried out 10,000 of the little knitted vests, made by ladies all over the UK and now used extensively as wool packing around the drugs and delicate medical equipment of ECHO's goods.

'There is so much we could report on,' they said, 'but, in conclusion, the thing that came over to us most was the absolute totality of the relief workers' dedication to what they are doing in Ethiopia. The love that was given to the Ethiopians in such dire need was, we felt, an example of what God's love is for us, and it is through these workers who are totally dedicated to what they are doing that God's love will flow to the underprivileged. These people may be poor, and their clothes like cobwebs, but through all this they retain a dignity that is far greater than we have ever seen. The faces and the eyes particularly, are so beautiful, and the smile comes through. It was an experience we would never have missed and one that will remain with us for the rest of our lives.'

The battle against Africa's famine will continue, and will not disappear quickly, even if sufficient aid reaches its victims. Whole families may never be able to return to their home villages unless sufficient help is made available to rehabilitate their land; all in all, the picture is grim. The drought brought a human tragedy of gigantic proportions. Yet, in the face of these terrible odds, the courage of the people was astonishing. What else could we do but make their needs our priority? Unless there is investment in agriculture and livestock, in wells and irrigation, these tragedies will certainly recur every few years.

Overall, Africa is failing in its ability to feed itself. One positive effect of these crisis could be to make the world realise the fact and take steps to ensure that it is no longer acceptable for people to die from lack of food.

The scale of need is far beyond the scope of all the voluntary agencies combined. The involvement of governments and international bodies, in funds, rehabilitation and land development and long-term development programmes is absolutely vital to ensure that the people are less vulnerable to the ravages of periodic drought. It will also be essential to make good provision to help the population with medical services and field hospitals maintained by doctors and nurses from other countries. In the meantime, more vehicles and aircraft are needed so that supplies can be taken to inaccessible areas. Irrigation schemes are being built up and must further develop, to assist in food production, together with the distribution of seeds, fertilisers and agricultural tools to help people in the continuing recovery programme. In some areas, however, we have to realise that work and development of relief efforts is badly hampered by civil war, social unrest and arms bills. But while the struggle to survive still grips some areas, others give better news. Happy, strong children come to centres for check-ups and to help carry the family rations back to their villages.

Despite their suffering, however, Ethiopian Christians continue to spread the Gospel courageously, whenever and wherever they can. In better times, funerals, for instance, used to be considered by Christian families as a prime evangelistic opportunity. Now, the Church is forbidden to use Christian burial rites, to plant a cross on a grave or even to sing!

A young Christian man at the funeral of his mother preached the Gospel and his brothers sang. After the ceremony he was arrested and thrown into jail. Another Christian was arrested for holding a prayer group in his house.

Some 1,500 churches out of 2,700 have been closed in one denomination alone, and it is estimated that more than 200 pastors have been imprisoned. All in all, some 80% of all churches are now closed, but the Gospel is spreading and people are being won for Christ with more than 600 believers in one particular area.

May God give each of us the love of Jesus in our hearts. He saw the people and was oft-times overwhelmed, but He always saw people as people.

20 : Growing out of all proportion

With many new and exciting programmes being planned for the future support of Christian Medical Missionary endeavour and relief work, ECHO was now growing at an alarming rate. We were now working with most of the world's agencies dedicated to the relief of human suffering.

Nearly two thousand mission hospitals in Third World countries were now facing financial problems, with rising costs of medicine and medical equipment reflected in rising costs to the patients. Also, as more and more mission hospitals were coming under national leadership, the replacement of missionary personnel by salaried national doctors and nurses, caused a severe drain on hospital resources. It must be remembered that missionary personnel were sent out by supporting missionary societies and churches, at no expense to the receiving hospitals. In many poorer nations few, if any, grants could be paid to these hospitals because of extreme poverty severely affecting Third World medical budgets. All this put a great strain on the financial viability of mission hospitals which, in raising costs, tended to price out the truly poor.

It was with these problems in mind that in July 1975 the ECHO Development Trust had been created to support the development of ECHO's services and to assist medical missionary endeavour worldwide.

In 1983, the ECHO Council of Management had agreed to free James from some of his duties as Medical Director, in order to serve as Development Officer of the ECHO Development Trust. He would spearhead a special appeal fund for the Trust. Following this decision, James and I had launched into a programme of fund raising ideas. We had built up a team of co-ordinators all over the country; people who were enthusiastic to help in whatever way they could, by making ECHO known in their areas. Coffee mornings, bring and buy sales, sponsored events and public meetings. We designed Christmas cards, notelets and a calendars; we gave transparency talks and displays. One enthusiastic supporter started an ECHO stamp bureau; another a Webb Ivory agency. A certain church sang 'in concert' in many churches and halls in the south of England raising in total, nearly

£3000. Cliff Richard donated £5000 from the proceeds of one of his 'pop' concerts. These and many other activities indicated the wonderful support that was now behind the organisation to prepare for the tasks ahead.

The biggest challenge to the Trust, however, was the raising of the £500,000 Warehouse and Development Appeal Fund, described in chapter 17. This received such a generous response that it enabled ECHO to move into its present modern warehouse and headquarters at South Coulsdon, free of any commercial debts.

As a result of this appeal, a major grant from the Wolfson Foundation led to the rapid development of our technical services. It enabled specialist technical equipment to be added to ECHO's technical department, and we were also able to employ a further graduate engineer. This grant also meant that we were able to send technical staff to the Third World to help advise medical missionaries on all technical matters in the medical equipment field. One such visit to Tanzania with the assistance of a small plane and pilot of the Missionary Aviation Fellowship, enabled our head of technical services to visit seventeen mission hospitals in the space of six weeks, and to repair thirty major pieces of medical equipment that were lying idle through lack of expertise and spare parts to repair them.

On the question of spare parts for mission hospital equipment, the British Petroleum Company gave a generous grant to enable ECHO to supply all maintenance and replacement parts free of charge to missionary hospitals all over the world. Six hundred and seventy eight items were sent by air freight during the first year of the scheme. Once again God was providing for the needs of mission hospitals through ECHO, and the generous support of BP. This service has been an enormous encouragement to many mission hospitals. We pray that God will enable other new projects to materialise as missions and aid organisations increasingly turn to ECHO for support.

The ECHO reconditioned Land Rover service, initiated in 1985, was a further project that really took off. We decided to develop this service because of the popular requests for Land Rovers overseas, due to their versatility. A factory unit was set up where used Land Rovers could be completely rebuilt, fully reconditioned and refurbished as new, by specialist renovators. Vehicles -mainly fully equipped as Jungle Ambulances- were all guaranteed and offered at far below the cost of a new vehicle. Orders started to pour in and the factory became hard pressed to fulfil requirements, which meant increasing staff and doubling output. A simple idea in the first instance, blessed of God, it proved a tremendous help to struggling medical causes overseas. Even maintenance spares could be provided

A convoy of reconditioned Land Rovers for overseas

through the 'Spare Parts Scheme' and a large bank of spares had to be built up. There was need for one such Land Rover, especially equipped for a water drilling programme in the Ethiopian villages. Readers of the ECHO newsletter and other interested friends and groups, generously supplied the Land Rover, which carried the sign, 'Donated by Friends of ECHO' on its side.

A further new venture, created first at Ewell and developed as we moved to Coulsdon, was the creation of a Veterinary Division. Famine, drought and disease were affecting domestic animals in many lands and more and more aid organisations entered the field of animal husbandry. This in turn would help to provide food and a livelihood for people in these lands. As Veterinary Surgeons gave their services to Third World countries, they needed drugs, veterinary equipment, animal vaccines etc. Thus we entered into a new sphere of service, supplying a whole range of veterinary products to help combat animal disease, to help produce healthy livestock and to improve food resources in developing nations. Also, a secondary benefit of this service was to make an effective contribution towards reduction in human disease transmitted via animals, by treating the animal host.

By 1986, ECHO was the principal organisation in the world running such a specialised supply of service for medical missionaries. Supplies in the warehouse were held for nearly 2000 hospitals in 120 Third World countries. A whole range of appropriate technology medical equipment was now being designed and manufactured through British Industry for the Third World. We were also continuing to supply surplus medical equipment from British hospitals, which was completely rebuilt and refurbished as new in our own technical workshop.

However, we were conscious that a great responsibility would rest upon us in the days ahead. If ECHO was to be the principal source of medical equipment and supplies for the missionary hospitals of the world, we would have to continue to maintain equipment in areas separated by vast distances in the developing world; we would also have to continue to guarantee supplying maintenance spares for our equipment. But what use would spare parts be without trained technicians to replace these parts and to maintain the equipment in good running order? Considering these things, yet another vision emerged; a vision to establish small technical workshops in developing nations where national technicians could be trained to maintain and repair their own hospital equipment.

The first pilot 'Technical Workshop' was set up at Kampala in Uganda, as this was a land where military, economic and political disturbances had created enormous difficulties in maintenance and supply for the mission hospitals. A missionary engineer, after specialised training in the maintenance of medical equipment at ECHO, was sent out through the Church Missionary Society. Five giant steel containers had barred windows cut into them and were built on to a concrete base. Water and electricity were connected and the whole workshop complex thatched over for coolness. Through a generous grant from a Christian Trust, the ECHO Development Trust financed the equipping and setting up of the workshop, and one of ECHO's reconditioned Land Rovers was donated to the new technical project. When supplies and spare parts arrived from ECHO, together with a second missionary electrical engineer, the work of maintaining the medical equipment in Uganda hospitals developed fast, despite troubled conditions in the land. Later, a second workshop was set up in Tanzania, with a major emphasis on training national technicians to maintain equipment in the sixty six hospitals in Tanzania. This workshop was attached to Mvumi Hospital, with the help of Tear Fund and the Overseas Development Administration of the UK government and the EEC.

The first course of ten weeks started in 1990, training a group of resident students in the maintenance of hospital equipment. This was a workshop where 'dead' hospital equipment would be restored to life and where maintenance men from hospitals all over the country would come to be trained.

At the end of the course each student received a tool kit and returned with it to the rural hospitals from which they came, confident and equipped to put their training into practice. Hospital equipment which had lain broken and unused for months, came to life again under their care.

Further workshops will need to be started by ex-patriot missionary engineers, but as soon as national technicians are sufficiently trained, they will pass into national leadership, and will just have the back-up service of ECHO.

More new developments were planned and further professional staff recruited. Miss Carolyn Green MPS, an experienced missionary pharmacist, came to help in the complicated task of pharmaceutical supply of basic generic drugs to developing countries, and to control the complex regulations and quality control of sending drugs to 120 nations overseas.

Then came Dr John Townsend, FRCS. After a distinguished career as Surgeon Administrator at Manorom Christian Hospital in Thailand with the Overseas Missionary Fellowship, and six years as Medical and Health Care Consultant to the British Tear Fund, he now came to work as Deputy Medical Director to James. This was with a view to replacing James in 1988 as Medical Director.

Mr Keith Slatter, FCA, was to be the new Financial Controller. He was one of the original Trustees of the ECHO Development Trust, whilst also working as Financial Secretary of the Methodist Missionary Society. His considerable experience in missionary finance was to be a great asset to the finances and administration of ECHO. In 1991 Keith became ECHO's Chief Executive !

New staff and new tasks, however, meant that ECHO's headquarters would need to be enlarged. So in 1986 builders moved in to add a two storey extension to the present building (the fourth headquarters), and to create urgently needed new offices and facilities to expand services even further. Staff had now increased over the years from three to seventy-five, now operating in many departments under the supervision of the Chief Executive, the Medical Director and the Departmental Managers. ECHO was growing out of all proportion at an alarming rate !

....oOo....

21 : Final months at ECHO

During 1988 a special conference was held at the headquarters of the Church Missionary Society, to address the problem of the CRISIS facing the church related hospitals in many Third World countries. Delegates attended from many missionary societies and Christian organisations, including national Church leaders from overseas.

Many fine missionary hospitals with long traditions of service, were now finding it harder to carry on. National economic problems and extreme poverty of the people severely affected the viability of their work.

The ECHO Development Trust had been created back in 1975 in order to support the development of ECHO's services and to assist medical missionary endeavour worldwide. James had become Development Officer of the Trust, and was now given the task of raising £200,000 annually, to lessen the burden of those who were in service in Christian hospitals in many parts of the world. Apart from the general development fund, five other special funds were created to cover freight, AIDS, disasters, Land Rovers and a discretionary fund to enable ECHO to respond to special crisis needs.

Together with other major British agencies, ECHO was invited to participate in the work of a newly created AIDS consortium, set up to combat this deadly disease which was now emerging in so many countries. This deadly virus infection was spreading rapidly and was particularly serious in many African countries. One survey revealed that in a Ugandan hospital no less than 20% of expectant mothers were tested positive for AIDS and it was estimated that at least half of the babies born to these women would be infected, many having no more than a year or two to live. This was a tragedy of unrivalled proportions to countries already struggling with economic and other health problems. Patients suffering from AIDS were coming to the hospitals in great numbers and the medical workers had little facilities to test for the HIV virus which often spread through blood transfusions, inadequately sterilised syringes etc. But today, AIDS testing kits are supplied by ECHO at a special low price, and these are enabling medical teams to identify AIDS sufferers and carriers; also making sure that blood for transfusion is not contaminated.

1988 was our last year before we were due to retire from ECHO and it was no less active than any of the previous 22 years had been. At the beginning of the year we travelled to the Gambia in West Africa where we spent two wonderful weeks re-visiting the land which had meant so much to us in years gone by. Many were the nostalgic thoughts that passed through our minds as we penetrated into the interior on safari through the forest and savannah, and canoed through the mangrove swamps. One of the most exciting contacts we had, was one with the Gambian Government officials. We discussed the news of a one million dollar grant from the World Health Organisation, through the World Bank. Most of this was to be spent at ECHO for many of the drugs needed in the Gambian Health Programme. Because of the economy of the Gambia, there was a desperate need for drugs at this time.

ECHO's drugs in the Gambia

We also took news to the Methodist Missionary Society working in the Gambia. The World Council of Churches in Geneva had made a grant to them of £30,000. This was earmarked for drug consignments for the medical work of the mission in this country. We were welcomed with open arms! We spent some time up-country visiting the Marakisa Medical Clinic, also the Medical Research Centre at Fajara, just outside Banjul. Everywhere we went the story was the same; lack of drugs and lack of finance to procure them.

At the end of March we left for an extensive tour of the Central States of America; the main object of the visit being to promote ECHO amongst the churches and mission headquarters in Chicago, Gulfport, Indianapolis, New Orleans and Memphis. In all these places we met vital medical contacts. The whole tour was worthwhile and beneficial.

There were floods in the Sudan during the year, which had left one and a half million people homeless. ECHO responded for all the major Aid organisations, airlifting relief supplies of tents, reinforced polythene sheeting to create makeshift tents, water containers, water purifying tablets and £95,000 worth of drugs and medical equipment needed to combat a disaster of this magnitude. Staff worked long hours to complete this operation and hardly had they completed it than the next disaster struck. This time floods in Bangladesh. Twenty eight million water purifying tablets and many other medical requests were rushed out to their aid.

Relief supplies awaiting airlift to a disaster area.

But probably the worst disaster of the year happened in December when there was a terrible earthquake in Armenia, Russia. So once again, just hours after news of the worst disaster to hit this region for 1000 years, reached this country, a load of £400,000 worth of vitally needed medical equipment and drugs were supplied to the British Red Cross, the Russian Red Cross, Save the Children Fund, the Daily Mirror and Nipon Japanese TV. The whole operation was recognised, acknowledged and thanked by the British government, with a personal letter from Mrs Margaret Thatcher, who was Prime Minister at that time, acknowledging ECHO's role in the nation's response.

This disaster was, infact, a break through of enormous importance. It was the first chink in the Iron Curtain, as Russia called and accepted help from the West, into the Eastern European Bloc countries. Although we were not aware of it at the time, it was also the first insight that we, personally, were to experience to stimulate our thoughts and interest in these countries.. The Lord was, in fact, opening our eyes to consider His people and their needs in

Relief supplies being unloaded

an area where Christianity had been banned for seventy years.

As we reminisce over the past years we realise that the way has not been easy. It has been a continuous journey of ups and downs, with much chastening along the way. We have, however, been conscious of the power of the Holy Spirit in our lives throughout and have endeavoured to give God all the glory for the privilege of serving Him through exhilarating experiences of impossibilities and miracles. For surely these were the kind of occasions that lifted us out of the deep valley times we had also experienced along the way.

James was not without his physical problems. He had to choose the week we were moving house to develop a kidney stone! This involved emergency action and a rapid alteration of plans. He was out of action for a few weeks, but soon recovered to leap into action once more. Shortly afterwards he visited Kenya to discuss the setting up of a pharmaceutical service with mission hospital representatives. He then flew on to Tanzania to visit further mission hospitals including Mvumi Hospital of Jungle Doctor fame. Here he made preliminary plans for the setting up of the technical workshop scheme mentioned in the previous chapter.

In March, following the severe winter of that year, we took off for Bermuda to spend a glorious fortnight with friends, utilising the time to fit in a series of ECHO engagements, and so enthusing another area of the world in the activities of the organisation.

We returned to a busy round of deputation meetings during the spring, to be followed by a spate of garden parties in our new home. We were in full flight again and now had a certain amount of freedom that we never had when running a guest house and conference centre. At the same time, my elderly mother had been living with us for more than 20 years and, as she was entering her nineties, although still very active, she needed more supervision and attention and was becoming more and more dependent upon us. The strain and responsibility of this situation, together with our involvement with so many activities and interests, was beginning to tell on me, although I did not realise it at the time. Whatever I was doing, I never felt relaxed and was always on the 'Listen'. At the same time, to satisfy my frustration, I got involved in many unnecessary things. In a sense, this was to excuse myself of the responsibility I knew was mine.

ECHO was developing fast and growing apace, and it was necessary to put more effort into this area too, as well as my considerations and responsibilities to my mother. Eventually I had to give up my days at ECHO because she could not be left alone. I performed my ECHO responsibilities at home, as far as I could, and this situation was to continue until her ultimate death in July 1989. But despite these difficulties, we were full swing into outreach for ECHO, up and down the country, church activities and interests and various local commitments. Kind friends 'Nannie sat' where possible, to enable us to get around. At the same time, years were catching up on us and our natural and physical abilities were beginning to wane a little now! We read in *Isaiah chapter 30 verse 15*: 'In repentance and rest is your salvation, in quietness and trust is your strength, but you would have none of it.'... This is how it was with me, and I enjoyed being the centre of attention in my busyness. Times with the Lord were taking second place and generally, I was spiritually 'out of breath'. I sought spiritual healing and ministry in this area, but did not immediately deal with the counsel and advice I had sought.

Then the Lord spoke to me in no uncertain terms. Another heart attack whisked me abruptly into hospital, and we were forced to place 'Nannie' in a home where she eventually died at the age of 97. A week later the situation worsened and I landed up in the Intensive Care Unit. As a Christian, I knew that my future was secure, but when I came face to face with that future, the human part of me began to battle against the spiritual certainty, and there was that moment of hesitancy which I find impossible to explain. I was conscious of my heart literally thumping underneath a false facade. But then, as I lay amidst the wires and tubes of the Cardiac Care Unit and thought about Jesus and about God, I felt a wonderful sense of peace. I knew hundreds of people were praying and this gave me a tremendous sense of support and encouragement.

Never consider you are wasting your time when you pray for someone. Maybe you think that there are so many praying, that your small offering is unnecessary; never think that way. The more prayer, the stronger the support.

A week or so later, after the crisis, further spiritual ministry for healing leaves me with little to say; it was a very special time. There was no dramatic healing, no visions, but I knew the Lord was very real and present in this situation, and I was confident that healing would take place, even if the process took time. By God's grace it had happened before; it could happen again. I would thank and praise the Lord every day, confident that one day, my heart checks would be back to normal again. This whole experience had been a lesson that I had to learn. As Christians we have to realise that we can be 'too busy for God' if we are not careful and when this happens we need to stop and think. Is it not more important to keep so close to Jesus in our earthly pilgrimage that we can be of greater use and value in our service for Him? Sometimes we have to learn the hard way!!.

Indeed, three months later after all this drama, we were able to leave for West Africa for a time of convalescence, to be combined with some visitations to mission stations on behalf of ECHO. Undoubtedly, I had experienced the divine touch of God's hand of healing as I slowly regained strength again.

There are bound to be times when God leads us through dark valleys in order to reach the mountaintop pastures of His love. We knew that these experiences of exhilaration and thrilling advancement of ECHO could never have been possible unless we had been prepared to trust our Lord with a measure of strong determination and faith in the dark and often difficult valley experiences.

Never doubt the Lord's dealings with you; remember, God knows best. Do not be despondent if you have setbacks when you are waiting for God to answer your prayers, but press on, praise God and never give up. What happens to us isn't nearly as important as how we react to what happens.

....oOo....

22 : To God Be The Glory

By 1989 ECHO was serving over 3500 medical concerns in 120 countries of the developing world, involving 500 missionary societies and charities. The budget had now reached £7 million and there were 70 staff on the team.

As we looked back over 23 years, we remembered those early days when a simple vision stirred in our hearts. We had experienced severe medical shortages in Africa; we had seen quantities of medical equipment in the UK. Why not link the two? This was a vision from the Lord and we must obey that vision regardless of the cost. But in those early days we never imagined that our tiny organisation with a 'converted stable' headquarters, a staff of three and a budget of £7000 would grow into an international Christian medical supply agency, playing a significant role in the relief of human suffering worldwide.

During those 23 years there were many exciting moments but one of the most exciting highlights, for us personally, really was a mountaintop experience in the pasture of God's love. It was the tremendous privilege, in 1984, of seeing ECHO recognised in the Queen's Birthday Honours, when James was presented with the Order of the British Empire, for the creation and development of the Equipment for Charity Hospitals Overseas.

It was all very exciting as with our two daughters, Josephine and Rosemary, we entered the Palace. The splendour and magnificence of all the pomp and ceremony is something none of us will easily forget. The gold trappings and plush red velvet; the crystal chandeliers, magnificent paintings and exquisite tapestries of the ballroom. All was just more than one can accurately portray in words. The statue-like forms of the lifeguards in the foyer; the bodyguard 'Beefeaters' and the band of the Welsh guards in the balcony. It all added to the grandeur of the occasion, and created a sense of serene beauty which gave the impression of another world.

The recipients filed in one by one and each had an audience with the Queen. It was a tremendous honour for James to be able to share briefly (he was not lost for words!) the ongoing work of ECHO and to recognise the apparent interest Her Majesty showed. It was a proud moment for the girls and myself, as we watched the whole ceremony in awe and admiration. It passed through our imaginative minds how much greater would be the grandeur when we finally met in the presence of the King of Kings.

So in July 1989 James and I officially retired from ECHO; from the work that had meant so much to us both. After 23 years we were no longer to be in control of 'our baby'; we felt strange to say the least! It did not prove easy to 'let go' after so many years, but we had to let others take up the reins now, and follow the Lord towards the next step.

Throughout the years, we had experienced the hand and blessing of God upon ECHO as it had steadily developed in the service of a very needy world. So we left ECHO in the hands of a dedicated team of workers and competent leadership, confident that they would lead ECHO forward into the years ahead.

Then came another exciting and surprising highlight. Soon after our official retirement from ECHO, James was recognised as the winner of the individual 'Templeton' UK award for 1989. This award is "A mark of recognition and encouragement for making a single contribution to the field of spiritual values in the United Kingdom." It was given to James "For services to the developing world."

James receiving the Templeton Award from Lord Tonypandy with Peggy and daughter Josephine

The author and family at Buckingham Palace when James received the OBE in recognition of his services in creating and developing ECHO (left to right) Rosemary, Peggy, James and Josephine.

The Templeton Award, an international prize for progress in religion, was instigated by Sir John Templeton in 1972. It has established itself as one of the world's major prizes. We felt humbled and inadequate that such an honour should be bestowed upon us, but also, we were so thrilled that God's work had been recognised. At the same time we realised that it was "To God be the glory, great things He had done."!

In the absence of His Royal Highness the Duke of Edinburgh, who was the usual presenter of the award, a special ceremony was organised in Cardiff to be conducted by Lord Tonypandy. This was indeed another memorable occasion for us, as we shared with the organisers of the Templeton Award, all that God had accomplished through ECHO over the years, in the service of a very needy world.

Thus we left the exciting experiences of the formation of ECHO on a highlight, surely one of the most thrilling mountaintops of God's love. But God had not finished with us yet.

....oOo....

23 : Into retirement

Now, as we contemplated a new lifestyle in retirement, we prayed that God would clearly reveal to us what He wanted us to do. We did not feel like spending the rest of our earthly pilgrimage just indulging in the things we had never had time to consider; this way of spending our latter years did not attract us at all!

Just one year before our retirement from ECHO, James had been asked to take up appointments with the Medical Missionary Association. Little did we realise then, that these appointments were to have far reaching effects on our future. For many years he had served on the Council of this Association; since our return from Africa in 1956, infact. For a while he had also become their acting Chairman, so he was very familiar with their work. He had, himself, been trained and helped through the Edinburgh Medical Missionary Society (EMMS), which is a very similar organisation to the MMA. This was when he was studying medicine at Edinburgh University during the war years, as he prepared for missionary service overseas.

Then in 1988 came the tragic death of Dr Stanley Browne, who was President of the Association at that time. He had been one of the world's foremost Leprologists and had made an outstanding contribution to the knowledge and treatment of leprosy. So it was that James was now elected as the next President of the MMA, by his colleagues on the Council. This was indeed a great honour, but he was very conscious that this appointment would not be easy. Infact it was going to be an almost impossible task to follow in the footsteps of such distinguished medical missionaries as Sir Clement Chesterman and Dr Stanley Browne, the two former Presidents.

In 1989 a special conference was called by the MMA Council to sort out and discuss the many decisions that would have to be made for the future role of the Association. So, Council members, Vice Presidents and many leading medical missionaries met together under James' leadership to discuss future aims and possible activity changes. It was necessary to consider medical students, medical missionaries and the medical missionary involvement of the church as a whole. All these areas were still vitally important and vitally needed. So, as a result of this specific conference, much prayer and heart searching penetrated through the Council members as together, they searched for God's will for the future role of the Medical Missionary Association.

The Medical Missionary Association is one of the oldest missionary organisations in the UK. For over 120 years it has taken an active role in the whole medical missionary work of the Christian Church. Throughout that time it has been assisting men and women who are preparing to go overseas as medical missionaries, for every section of the Christian Church.

Today however, the pattern of medical missionary work throughout the world is changing and there are many problems amongst mission medical centres overseas. For instance, when missionary doctors are due for furlough, or need short periods off for further training, often there are no doctors to replace them.

Although at this point James was privileged to play a leading role in the affairs of the MMA as President and acting Chairman, he still had his own small medical practice, so could not be as actively involved with the Association as he would have liked. Nevertheless, he spent much time considering how missionary doctors could be relieved for their furlough breaks and study periods. Finally, with the approval of the MMA Council, he decided to think about launching a campaign. Why not challenge Christian doctors in the UK and other Western nations, to face up to the tremendous opportunities and needs in so many Third World situations today. Would it be possible for them to give some of their time to help in some way? Perhaps in retirement to offer 3-6 months of their time and expertise. In any case, such possibilities would at least allow missionary doctors to get their necessary furlough, or time off for post graduate studies and further training.

The more we thought about all this, the more we considered our own situation. What was stopping us "setting the ball rolling"? James was now free of his ECHO responsibilities, his medical practice could be taken care of for a short spell, and I was so wonderfully restored to health again. What was there to hold us back? Also, as President of the MMA, James thought that by heading up the campaign, by going overseas himself for a short spell, he would be in a better situation to challenge other doctors to offer their services for brief periods too.

So we started to plan. Who would like us for three months? Several requests came to us. The first was from the Sudan Interior Mission. Could we go to their station, ELWA, near Monrovia in Liberia? Two of the doctors working at the hospital needed to get away to Kenya for a few weeks, to attend an 'All Africa AIDS Conference' being held there. Unless replacements could be found, they would not be able to go. With the growing problem of AIDS worldwide, it was essential that medical personnel, particularly those working in remote areas, should be well informed.

Then we had a call from South Africa to visit Kwa Zululand. Could we go to co-ordinate with the Minister of Health as to the medical needs of help in that country? Also, the MMA had been asked to help in staffing the former mission hospitals in Kwa Zulu.

As we were considering these two requests and the possibilities of helping both, political disturbances in Kwa Zulu and neighbouring territories made us decide to shelve the South African request for the time being! So we settled for three months in Liberia.

S.I.M. ELWA Liberia, Mission Station.

Our adventure started on a cold, frosty January morning in 1990. We passed over Morocco and on down the west coast of Africa and the western Sahara. Not a tree in sight not even a blade of grass, only mile after mile of sand. Here and there we spied an oasis, just an isolated patch of water surrounded by scanty scrub. The whole scene was bathed in brilliant sunshine and shrouded in a misty haze of red sand dust. As we glanced over the calm, deep blue sea, we noticed little pin prick boats on the glassy surface. It was all so exciting and beautiful.

On to Senegal, the Dakar peninsula, the Gambia, Guinea Bissau and Sierra Leone. From our frozen start to 32° in a matter of hours! Now, the desert blended into scrub land, red sandstone roads and thin forest areas. Then, as we approached Liberia and began to descend, we saw the mangrove swamps, tall palm trees and scattered small African villages. So to Monrovia airport, typical of Africa with the usual hustle and bustle, babbling crowds and dust!! It was all there; we were back in Africa.

....oOo....

24 : Eternal love winning Africa

So, here we were in Liberia, having come to set in motion the idea of creating an exciting extension to MMA's ministry. In this case we were trying to demonstrate the value of sharing a lifetime of medical experience in some small way, with the desperate healthcare needs in the poorer nations of the world. At the same time, relieving those doctors already hard pressed and wearied by the mere pressure of their responsibilities.

As we entered the airport terminal, there was Philip Wood, one of the doctors that James was coming to relieve. As he directed us out to the waiting ELWA transit van, we were very aware of the hot, humid atmosphere. We were also aware of armed soldiers, complete with tin hats and rifles!

"What's all this about Philip?" enquired James.

"There's been some political disturbances up country," replied Philip, "Dissidents and a military coup has caused an alert, with road blocks everywhere and strict identity overall. We are hoping they don't get any further than an alert."

But it was more than an alert. There had already been many killings and many Liberians had fled from their villages to neighbouring Ivory Coast and Guinea. This was a good start for us, we thought. We had avoided Kwa Zulu because of the unrest there, then the day we set foot in Liberia, we found political unrest here too!!

ELWA (Eternal Love Winning Africa) is a large mission station of the Sudan Interior Mission. It is situated on the Atlantic coast, with about 100 acres of land. It caters for all the other SIM stations in West Africa, so there is always much coming and going of missionaries.

In this hot and humid tropical climate, we soon learnt to appreciate the warm Atlantic breezes and the cool sound of the gigantic ocean rollers as they beat upon the sandy shore. How good to experience the call of the birds as they flashed from one coconut palm to another, and the chirruping crickets hidden in the rough undergrowth. Then, at this time of the year there were the turtles that popped their heads above the water from time to time, and the little crabs frantically digging holes, then tossing the sand into the air before scurrying off in pursuit of something or the other. One of these little chaps got into our apartment one day and gave us quite a start as it skidded across the floor! Then of course it wasn't long before we met up with the enormous mahogany African cockroaches, with their antennae continually wafting in the breeze! How well we remembered these from our Congo days; scary fellows!!

There was a radio centre at ELWA, that daily beamed out the Gospel message to many remote African areas. There was also an excellent publishing centre on the compound and an Academy catering for 150 children from missionary and government families, and more affluent Liberian families.

Then of course, there was the hospital; a constant hive of sick people, the wards always full, with hundreds more patients waiting to be seen. From the very start, James found his time fully occupied with ward rounds and routine clinics. There were acute overcrowding situations everywhere, despite the fact that all surgical cases were sent home within two days where possible.

Morning by morning hundreds of patients crowded into the outpatients department to be screened by the Liberian PA's (physician's assistants) These PA's were specially trained to diagnose and treat common ailments; serious cases were transferred to the doctors. Emergencies frequently interrupted any routine; caesarean sections, strangulated hernias and accidents. How much so many of these cases reminded us of our days in Africa forty years previously, except here there was more equipment with which to tackle such cases. There was also good laboratory and pharmacy facilities, well stocked and organised.

Before entering into this 'retirement' experience, James had had a little surgical re-training but, he confessed, "Nothing they taught me prepared me for the sort of abdominal and gynaecological surgery they get out here."

There were so many acute abdomens, with massive generalised peritonitis, enormous infected cysts full of pus, where a good drain was needed and not always available; we had seen it all before! How often, in those early days we had resorted to a sliced up rubber glove! Hysterectomies were common place, with massive fibroids, often big enough to fill the whole abdomen. Ectopic pregnancies came in most days, often in a state of severe shock from rupture, or from massive internal haemorrhage.

Children came into outpatients daily, with tragic conditions of cerebral malaria, severe gastroenteritis, dehydration and malnutrition. There were cases of neo-natal tetanus that were too advanced to save. Many more

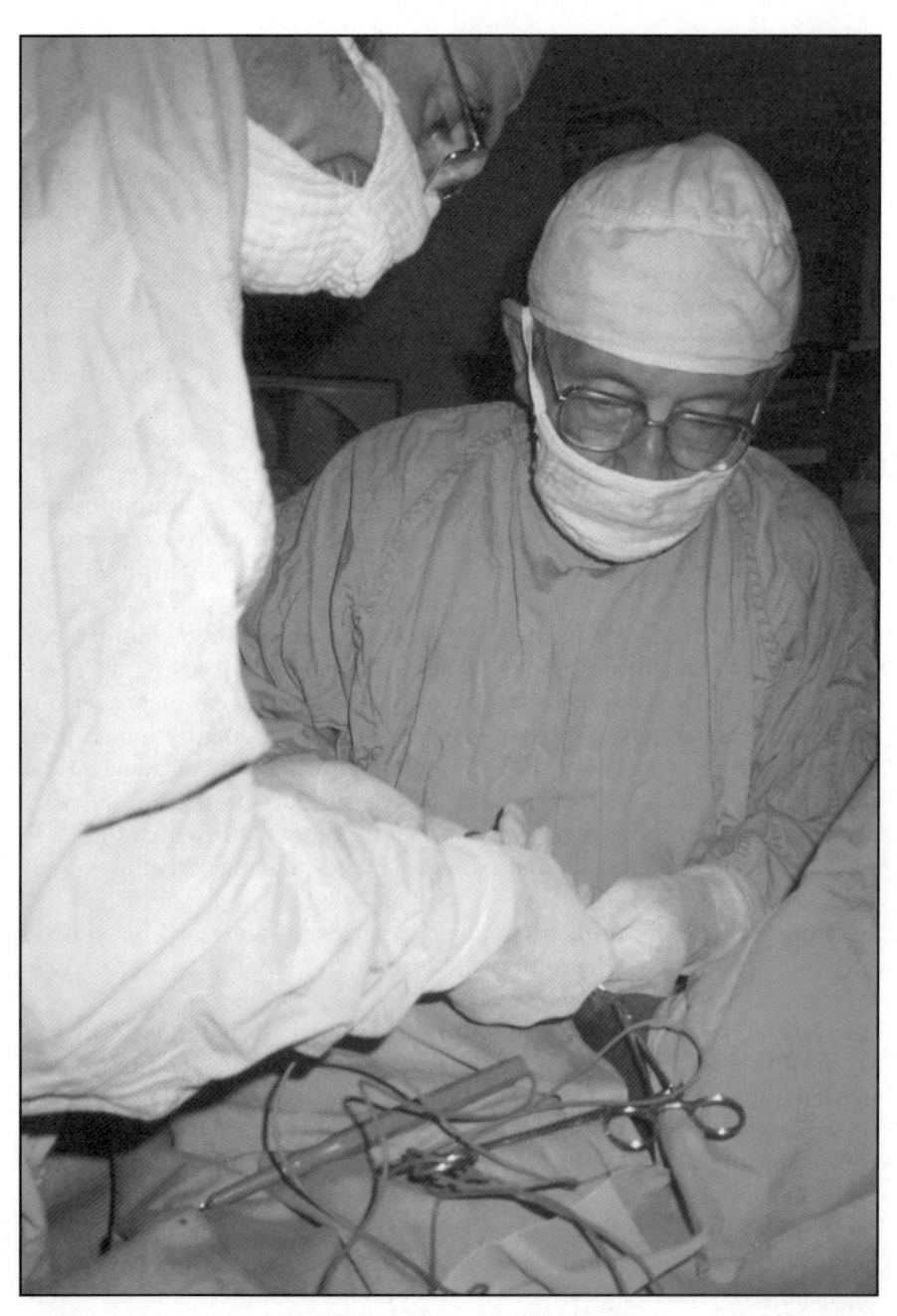

James operating in Liberia during his short term 'retirement' visit.

children died because they were brought in too late, often having been treated with village medicines and customs first. Some babies arrived suffering from 'rice stuffing' which meant that they had been force fed with rice, which often led to aspiration pneumonia.

One day James examined a little wizen bundle of a child. He was $1\frac{1}{2}$ years old and weighed just over 4 kilos. He was desperately ill with dehydration, gastro enteritis and cerebral malaria, and was admitted to the ward for urgent, life-saving intravenous feeding and drugs.

"Where is that child?" James enquired when he visited the ward later in the day.

"The parents would not stay." replied the Liberian nurse. This desperately ill child had been taken back to his village home to die. How sad, when we had all the help that was available, at least to make an all out effort to save this little scrap of humanity.

Being on the receiving end of medical needs sent out from ECHO gave us a tremendous thrill. Yes, it had been worth all the toil and sweat, as we looked back over those early years of ECHO's development. Our time in Liberia had certainly proved the value of ECHO's work and the need for its services. We noticed in particular, the baby incubators and the AIDS testing kits. ELWA Hospital was the only place in the whole of Liberia that could give safe blood transfusions, because of these special kits from ECHO, thus contributing in the help needed to halt the alarming spread of AIDS that is taking place in Africa today.

As we experienced at first hand, the tremendous needs and opportunities of Christian medical service at ELWA, our thoughts were continually being drawn back to the future work of the Medical Missionary Association. The tragic needs that we were experiencing could be multiplied a thousand times in so many poorer countries around the world. Was this a new challenge that we could place before the MMA on our return?

Having spent 23 years building up ECHO, supplying medical equipment and drugs to mission hospitals worldwide, we now began to see the need for more personnel in the future, to assist the young churches overseas in their overwhelming health problems. Somehow, these desperate medical needs of the Third World **must** reach and challenge Christian health professionals in the UK. How could the MMA fit into all this?

Now we began to realise a little more how the Lord had been training and preparing us through the years. Were we ready to take on the challenge?

During our time at ELWA we were thrilled to meet two medical students doing their medical school 'elective' training. They were experiencing at first hand how valuable a short period working in a mission hospital could be in their future careers.

James and Phillip off at the start of a days work at ELWA Hospital.

For many years, part of the MMA's work has been to give grants to medical students enabling them to do 'elective' periods in a missionary hospital. Time and time again these 'elective' periods have proved a life changing experience to young Christian undergraduates. Many missionary doctors now serving the Lord in different parts of the world, owe the initial call to their 'elective' experiences. It passed, through James' fertile mind whether this long standing ministry of the MMA should be extended to offer this opportunity to undergraduate nursing students too. He would look into the possibility when we returned home.

The military coup died down a little after a week or two of our arrival, but flared up again a couple of weeks before we were due to leave. This time two American missionaries were attacked and killed and hundreds of villagers too. Many villages were burnt down and thousands of people fled the country. Although very little news filtered through, we understood that the Liberian army was retreating, which was not a healthy sign. This was all happening just 100 miles from where we were stationed at ELWA. We were not sorry that our stay was almost over! Chaos was beginning to stir and the airport revealed some confusion as people were preparing to get out of this war situation. We left on one of the last planes before the airport was bombed and totally destroyed and further refugees were forced to flee via the Ivory Coast. Then, as the rebels advanced on Monrovia, the capital of

Liberia, they entered ELWA en route and destroyed in their wake, the radio station, the hospital and many other mission buildings. Nothing but shambles remained.

However, despite the coup, a hepatitis outbreak amongst the missionaries, together with the humidity and heat, we managed to complete what we had gone out to do and we both kept well in the process!

So we started our retirement years with a bang and as we returned from Liberia, we had to consider what our next move was to be. After all, what is retirement without a spark of life?

....oOo....

25 : New opportunities

On our return from Liberia James was anxious to develop his thoughts to enlarge the ministry of the Medical Missionary Association, as their President. However, for the time being he had his medical practice to consider, so at this point could do no more than share his ideas with the MMA Council.

At the same time, it was natural that our thoughts were still closely linked with the work of ECHO. We were still keen to 'know what was going on'. In particular, we could not forget that terrible earthquake disaster in Armenia, which was one of the last disaster situations in which we had been personally involved.

It so happened that some friends of ours were very familiar with this part of the world, and were very informative about the early days of the 'iron curtain' regime which were so difficult and often dangerous for the Christians of Eastern Europe.

Seventy years of atheism had brought the entire Soviet Union to economical, social, spiritual and moral bankruptcy and during the 1950's many churches had been confiscated by the Communists for preaching the Gospel. But today, the changes taking place in Russia and other Eastern Bloc countries have been truly amazing. People are back in the churches and there is a certain freedom that was never known during those restricted years. At the same time there is a desperate need for Bibles and Christian literature; the people are hungry for the Word of God.

Our friends shared this urgent need with us, and together we wondered whether there was anything we could do to help. For ourselves, we were becoming increasingly more anxious to be more integrated with the MMA, but for various reasons this was not yet possible or practical, other than thinking and listing a whole lot of ideas that may one day be applicable! Thus we were able to consider joining with our friends with their suggestions of helping with the supply of Christian literature for Russia.

So finally through a series of circumstances, together we created a new charity namely, 'The King's Highway Trust'. The main object of the Trust was to promote the publishing and distribution of Bibles and Christian literature in the countries of Eastern Europe. Pastors and congregations needed the Word of God; Christians young in the faith and women in the home needed other forms of Christian literature too. None of them had anything to encourage, nurture or train them in the truths of the Scriptures. The children too, needed teaching material that would help them to know the loving care of Jesus. Unanimously, we agreed that together we would aim to do what we could to help these brave young Christians in their faithful ministry.

A packed Church congregation in the Ukraine,

Through the generous support of a specific Trust and individual contributions, we soon started to accumulate funds which enabled us to start purchasing Russian Bibles. Further finance enabled us to begin writing, publishing and translating simple devotional study books, and special crayoning books, based on Bible stories for the children. Fund raising activities and various other events, all helped to finance our objectives. With James' previous experience of fund raising at ECHO, he made the ideal Chairman of the Trust, and was able to sandwich this side of the project between his other responsibilities without too much involvement.

Four visiting Pastors from the Ukraine.

    One particular highlight remains in my mind. During our contact with a particular Pastor working in the Ukraine, we heard about four other Pastors working in that land, under very difficult circumstances. They had all left secular jobs to preach and sing the Gospel message of God's love. Between them they were visiting 97 churches on a regular three month basis and travelled hundreds of miles to towns and villages where there was no Christian witness. The King's Highway Trust felt stirred to support these faithful servants of the Gospel in some way, so we invited them over to Britain and arranged a three week itinerary for them. From the moment they arrived the whole venture was an outstanding success, as they sang and gave testimony by interpretation at meetings up and down the country. They told of the desperate hunger of their people for the Word of God.

    "Have you got hunger for the Word of God?" they asked.

    "Then why do you have empty seats in your churches?"

    Everywhere people were blessed and stimulated by their sincerity and love. Gifts given throughout the itinerary enabled us to purchase a quantity of Bibles and Christian literature for them and we were also able to contribute a substantial amount towards their financial support. Finally, we found a suitable minibus and were able to present them with this, together with some loud speakers and musical instruments. These gifts would certainly help them to get out to the villages for open air meetings. But no one can forsee how much longer Pastors of such calibre as these, will be free to preach the Gospel in a land of unrest, and with such an uncertain future.

By the time The King's Highway Trust had been in operation for four years, it was developing fast. Although appointed as Chairman of the Trust, James was unable to give the time that he would like because of his medical commitments. Also, he was still anxious to develop his role as President of the MMA; it was impossible for him to fulfil all these things the way he would wish. In a sense, everything was becoming a little too much for all of us and some serious thinking, praying and considering had to be done. As we had learnt in the past, sometimes we are so busy doing the Lord's work that we forget to stop and listen to what He has to say!

So it was in 1994 that through a series of events and circumstances, we were able to link with the charity, 'Love Russia'. This Christian charity was serving Russia with humanitarian aid, as well as supporting and upgrading a number of orphanages. Infact, they were doing a wonderful work and displaying a very beautiful Christian witness to the people in that land. We felt guided to approach their Committee and after a series of necessary discussions, they graciously agreed to take on board the ministry of The King's Highway Trust. Thus the official merger took place on July 1st 1994 and we were all able to lay down the responsibilities of a rapidly developing work, in which we had been involved. We would continue to assist where we could, praying for the work of 'Love Russia' and promoting it wherever there were opportunities to do so. The idea of becoming more integrated with the Medical Missionary Association now began to look like a possibility!

With The King's Highway Trust being taken over and its work continued by 'Love Russia', James could now see the opportunity of taking a larger role in the affairs of the Medical Missionary Association. He had been their President since 1988, and for 6 years had led the Association as its acting Chairman. During these years the necessary development plans for the MMA had not materialised to any great degree, and this caused him some concern. As acting Chairman, he felt a deep burden of responsibility, but still with his other commitments, there was little he could do about it. He felt the urgent need for the Council to elect a London based Chairman, readily available to the MMA staff, responsible for the every day running of the Association. Therefore, he asked the Council if he could relinquish his position as acting Chairman. Mr Chris Lavy, a London based surgeon, graciously agreed to take James' place for 3 years. Before his term of office was complete however, he himself was to go overseas to serve in Malawi, but others followed on.

This wise step of laying down his responsibilities as MMA Chairman, now enabled James to give more time and thought to his position as President, and the future role God would have him carry out for the Association. He was only too aware of the fact that the need for medical missionaries was greater than ever, and he envisaged that God was now calling the Association to take radical steps of development to serve Christ and His Church worldwide.

We now sought to readjust our schedule and consider the future ahead. In the meantime, it was a question of waiting for the Lord to reveal to us how we could put into practice all the ideas and plans that James had in mind in his capacity as President of MMA.

During this time there was much heart searching and difficult decisions to make, but the various situations we found ourselves in during this waiting period, were going to be so valuable for our future commitments, even if we did not realise it at the time.

One situation, for example, involved us in major fund raising help for another Christian organisation that was setting up a new Centre for their ministry. With our future plans already under discussion, we could not possibly do much more than advise, although it was really exciting and a tremendous encouragement to see the new Centre acquired, then the following miraculous way that God provided finance, furnishings and staff, to set the whole project into action.

Otherwise, these intervening days were not easy. For a while we faced problems that we could not understand. 'Why does God give us these situations?' we thought. But we all have problems from time to time as we travel through life, and we just have to accept them and trust God, through the guidance of His Holy Spirit, to see us through. We have to realise that if we want to be true to our calling as followers of Jesus, we must be prepared for discipline and correction in one form or another.

So the next few months proved to be a great experience of faith and trust in a mighty God. We had a strong feeling that God was about to involve us in a greater service than we could ever have planned ourselves. From this time set aside, we were to emerge excited and enthusiastic about what was about to happen.

....oOo....

26 : Early years of the Medical Missionary Association

At this point we need to introduce you to the Medical Missionary Association in more detail. As we mentioned earlier, in Chapter 23, James had served on the Council of the MMA ever since our return from Africa in 1956, so he was very familiar with their work.

Now we felt the time had come to put another link in the chain. Thus we would be joining our pioneer medical missionary experiences in the Congo, to the supply ministry of ECHO and now on to the ministry of MMA. In so doing, we would be helping to support medical personnel called overseas to operate all the medical equipment sent abroad to Third World hospitals, dispensaries and disaster situations.

The Medical Missionary Association was founded in 1878. On March 2nd of that year seven men, five of them doctors, met in the London Medical Mission near Drury Lane. Their united ambition was to develop an Association that would concentrate entirely on medical missionary work. This would be a similar organisation to the Edinburgh Medical Missionary Society which had been formed 40 years before.

The meeting was a great success. This was to be the first organisation of its kind in London and was to be controlled by basic objectives as follows:-

"The promotion of real godliness amongst medical men and medical students, on the basis of the Holy Scriptures, by such means as may from time to time seem advisable, and to help forward such Christian work, both at home and abroad, as may properly lie within the spheres of medical agencies."

The policy of the new Association was not to become another missionary society, sending out its own missionaries, but to encourage and support existing societies.

So for the first seven years donations were given to support medical missionary endeavour, wherever there was a need. An informative magazine was published and various meetings were arranged for interested medical students. In those days practical social work among the poverty and sufferings of slum dwellers within Britain's cities was seen as the best training for the mission field.

In 1885 the Association was able to open a students' hostel in North London, where young Christian men involved in medical training could stay. These were students whose lives were committed to serve the Lord wherever He chose to send them. Many were infact, called to go overseas after their training.

Dr James L. Maxwell became the first Warden of the hostel. Together with his wife they integrated their home into the hostel and created a family like atmosphere amongst the students. Dr Maxwell was also Secretary of the MMA at the time. Originally he had been involved with a medical work in Formosa, but had returned to England on health grounds. Infact, he was one of the seven men who had met at that very first committee in 1878.

However, there were no medical grants available in those days as there are today, so it was a tremendous help for the students to stay at the hostel for very moderate charges that the MMA made, often contributing towards their university fees too, in certain cases.

Dr. J. L. Maxwell
The General Secretary and first warden of the MMA student's hostel.

It soon became increasingly obvious that the hostel was proving too small for the growing number of students seeking accommodation. So in 1889 the whole operation moved to new premises in Highbury, London, where it remained for the next 50 years.

Part of the training experience of the young students was to be involved in some practical social work. There was much poverty and suffering amongst the slum dwellers in the great cities of Britain, and London was no exception.

At this time small, independent medical missions had started to make an appearance in some of the poorer areas of London. MMA realised that they could add to this scheme, and at the same time give opportunity to the students to have experience in the practical work that they needed. They would not only be involved in running a medical clinic, but would also have the opportunity to minister amongst the people and have Sunday School activities too. This whole experience would be very worthwhile for those students, who would anticipate running similar Christian medical missions abroad.

So the idea was discussed and put into action. The Clerkenwell and Islington Medical Mission was started and the whole scheme became a great success and a real encouragement to the students. Students were also attached to other Medical Missions such as Old Ford, Bethnal Green and Landsdown Place. Many hundreds of young medical students enjoyed the happy atmosphere of the hostel, some for just a few weeks and some for several years. All left in due course to follow their chosen careers. All sought to follow the Lord, which was one of the guiding lights of the hostel.

It was around this time, between the two world wars, that the MMA also opened a hostel for women in North London, but this was closed at the onset of the second world war, and never reopened until Harcourt House in Canonbury opened.

Students coming into the hostel did not need to consider their denominational backgrounds. All were included and there were many interesting and profitable debates with encouraging outcomes round the dinner table and in the common room. These young doctors were all one in Christ Jesus; all studying medicine in His name. They were training to take up their places for the Lord wherever He chose to send them.

During World War II however, the work of the MMA reduced considerably. The hostel was closed to students and was used to house homeless families. The committee continued to operate, making occasional grants to medial missions and Christian medical students, also producing a few news sheets from time to time.

However, ex-students now working as missionary doctors, continued to minister overseas, ever grateful for the time they had spent in the MMA hostel during their days of training. Many of these missionaries pioneered health services and many made great contributions to the knowledge of tropical medicine and disease.

It was through the untiring efforts of Dr Clement Chesterman, working with the Baptist Missionary Society at Yakusu in the Belgian Congo, that the cause and control of Typanosomiasis (sleeping sickness) was first discovered. In the early days, this disease had claimed the loss of many lives throughout the Congo and other parts of Africa.

Called home to the UK just before the Second World War, Dr Chesterman took over the medical work of the BMS as their Medical Director - a post that James was to take over from him on our own return from the Congo. - Then in recognition of his outstanding contribution to tropical medicine, Dr Chesterman received a Knighthood from the Queen - as have other outstanding medical missionaries - and Sir Clement Chesterman was to serve for many years as President of the Medical Missionary Association, guiding it through the centenary year in 1978.

However, the time had come for things to change dramatically for the MMA after the war. The hostel at Highbury was never reopened again; the homeless families remained and later the property was sold. A new era was about to begin.

....oOo....

27 : MMA advances through the years

With the closure of the hostel at Highbury after the war, it soon became clear that the need for an MMA hostel was as great as ever. Over the years so many young missionary doctors in training had relied upon the inspiration and encouragement they had found in the hostel atmosphere as they prepared for medical missionary service. So in faith, a large house in specious grounds was purchased in Chislehurst, Kent, and in 1947 the new MMA hostel was opened.

Dr and Mrs Harry Bennett, who had pioneered a hospital in the Sudan and had worked together in a hospital in Uganda were appointed to take over the responsibility of running the hostel. At the same time Dr Bennett was appointed to carry out the duties of Secretary of the MMA, a role he was to carry out with such distinction over the next 25 years. Many medical missionaries were never to forget the influence that 'Harry and Isobel' Bennett had on their lives as they trained for their future careers.

Harry and Isobel Bennett.

But it soon became apparent that the Chislehurst hostel was unpractical. It was too far from the London teaching hospitals where the medical students were to study, also, it involved unnecessary time and expense of travelling. So, in 1952 the whole MMA complex moved back to London. Through the help of the Evangelical Alliance, ideal premises were found at nos. 31 and 32 Bedford Place, near to the British Museum, for a very moderate rent. It proved to be a much more practical situation, being right in the centre of London and near to most of the teaching hospitals. So for the next 25 years successive generations of Christian medical students enjoyed the hostel as their home during their days of training.

The post war years were days of rapid change for the medical world, both in the UK with the introduction of the National Health Service and also in the medical missionary work in the developing countries overseas. The young medical missionary of the post war period was to face situations in the emerging young independent nations very different to his predecessors of a former colonial generation. He would need to go forth as a servant of the young churches overseas. One of the great advantages of living in an MMA hostel was that the students were able to meet other missionaries and were also frequently introduced to the current missionary scene. Many leading medical missionaries who have played such a great part in Christian healthcare worldwide, look back with gratitude to God for the formative years of their lives spent in the MMA hostel, where they had been made increasingly aware of God's call to serve Him overseas.

During 1964 a new initiative was born. This was the OYSTER scheme (One Year's Service to Encourage Recruiting) This scheme was to enable young doctors to spend one year finding out whether they were in the right calling or not. The OYSTER scheme was the brain-child of Dr Harry Bennett. He had encountered appalling suffering and dreadful medical cases whilst himself, working overseas. He had seen blindness on a vast scale, dying babies, deformed bodies, septic sores and disease of every kind. All these cases could be healed if only there were the medical helpers available. All together, it made him realise how great the need was for medical help overseas. Much of these things could not be envisaged unless actually seen; doctors should experience these desperate needs at first hand. Hence OYSTERS came into being.

Nazareth hospital in Israel had already adopted the principle of taking on ex-patriate workers for just one year. Many had gone back to join the permanent staff as a result. Others continued to take an active interest in the work. Many more had gone elsewhere as medical missionaries, as the Lord had called, just because of that initial years experience.

Also in the mid-sixties, with the increasing number of women medical students feeling the call of God to serve overseas, the MMA decided to open a second hostel in Canonbury Place, Islington in North London. It was named Harcourt House after Miss Harcourt who had been warden at the Highbury hostel from 1912 to 1933. The original idea was for Canonbury Place to be a hostel for Christian women medical students, but before long men were admitted too.

Dr and Mrs Harry Bennett were asked to take over the running of Canonbury and Dr and Mrs Richard Bird, who had spent a number of years working as missionaries in the Middle East, assumed responsibility for the Bedford Place hostel.

At the same time, the lease at Bedford Place hostel eventually drew to a close; there was a changing pattern in the life of the London medical students. There were new government grants available to them and alternative accommodation was also available. So it was decided to close the Bedford Place hostel and to concentrate the work of the MMA in the Canonbury headquarters.

Peter and Hope Green.

In 1975, after a quarter of a century of dedicated service to the Association, Dr and Mrs Bennett retired from the responsibilities with the Canonbury hostel. The Council now realised that they would have to appoint another Warden, if the hostel was to continue running efficiently. It was at this time that Dr Peter Green had recently returned from missionary service in Kenya, and was willing, together with his wife, Hope, to take on the position at Canonbury hostel. Dr Green had also served in the Edinburgh Medical Mission Hospital at Nazareth, and spent many years with the Church of Scotland serving in Kenya. Peter and James had been students at the Edinburgh Medical Missionary Society and had worked together in the Christian Union. Then in 1947, Peter had been Best Man at our wedding. So Peter and Hope Green became joint Wardens of the hostel, and at the same time, Peter acted as Secretary of the MMA. Together, they entered into the vital task of challenging young Christian medicals with the claims of Jesus

Christ on their lives and professions, to serve Christ and His Church in the developing world.

Peter and Hope with a group of MMA residents outside Harcourt House.

The last years of Peter and Hope's distinguished service to the MMA were, however, to be years of change. The lease on the Canonbury headquarters was running out and it was important to secure a freehold centre to act as both a student residence and headquarters for the Association. Thus began a search that was to lead to the ideal property in Camden, North London. It's purchase price was £300,000 and a further £200,000 would need to be spent to extend the property and adequately equip it for MMA's new home. Was there any way that this could be achieved without affecting MMA's financial reserves and adversely interfere with the ability of the Association to carry out its vital role in medical missionary endeavour? As the Council prayed over the matter, the clear call of God came to 'go forward'. So as the Association moved forward in faith, they were to see yet another miracle, once more proving that 'with God all things are possible.' - even a £ $\frac{1}{2}$ million project of faith!

The new freehold hostel and headquarters at Camden were officially opened with a service of Dedication and Holy Communion, taken be Revd Dr Stanley Thomas, on December 8th 1989. Dr Stanley Thomas, who had had a long and distinguished missionary career in India, and was at that time a member of the MMA Council, led a gathering of Council members and friends in praise and thanksgiving to God for His goodness and blessing on the MMA, in giving the Association its lovely freehold home.

Under the leadership of Dr Peter Green and his wife, Hope, the hostel began to fill with Christian students and medicals from overseas, even through the difficult period of modernisation, extension and redecoration. By the autumn of 1990, the new hostel was fully operational with a full compliment of students.

Through the wise financial planning and guidance of the Treasurer at that time, namely, Mr Alister Watson, this delightful freehold headquarters was bought, partially rebuilt, extended, modernised and completely paid for by the full opening date. Thus there was no diminution of MMA's resources, that were so badly needed in the service of worldwide medical mission. It was so good that Peter and Hope, who had carried the heavy burden of the supervision and planning of the new headquarters, were to see the whole operation established and fully functioning by the time of their own retirement in 1999.

....oOo....

*The New MMA Headquarters in Camden Road,
London before extension and renovation.*

28 : MMA at the crossroads

The MMA was now at the crossroads of its long history. In many parts of the world medical missionary work was changing dramatically as doors were closing and visas were becoming more difficult to obtain. We were sad to receive news from the Democratic Republic of Congo. We knew that country so well, but now war and political unrest had torn it apart, making it impossible for missionaries to serve in some of the areas. We remembered days of freedom when we had spent those early years of missionary service amongst happy and grateful people. At the same time, we could never forget the 29 missionary colleagues who had died as Christian martyrs in those tragic years of rebellion and strife.

The need for committed health professionals to serve alongside the young churches was greater than ever before. From all over the developing world came the call, "Come over and help us for we cannot manage alone." One disease alone caused us to seriously consider this desperate call for help. AIDS was rearing its ugly head, spreading throughout Africa and Asia and overwhelming hard pressed health services. There were urgent needs for men and women in all branches of the medical profession to offer themselves to serve Christ and His Church in its hour of need. Was God calling the MMA to rise to this challenge and begin a new era in its long and distinguished history? So, as one of the oldest missionary associations in the UK, the MMA Council decided that the time had come to radically review its activities in the light of present day world needs.

Ever since its formation in 1878, the Association had been following the aspirations of its founders, and at the centenary gathering in 1978, the Council had looked back with praise and thanksgiving over 100 years of God's blessings. Now, in the second century of its work, and fast approaching the new millennium, the activities of the Association would be about to change to match the transformation of medical missionary work.

The future of the new premises on Camden Road was a point in question. As medical missionary work was changing, so was medical training. For so many years the traditional hostels of the MMA had been places of preparation and assistance for the medical missionaries of the future, but now the question was. how necessary were these hostels in a changing world?

The prime work of the MMA over the past 120 years had always been to prepare and support students for medical missionary work. It had also sought to encourage and support the medical missionary interests of the Church. Now, it seemed possible that God was directing the Council to consider expanding the ministry of the MMA. Why not challenge **all** Christian members of the health profession; nurses, dentists, physiotheropists etc; as well as doctors, to serve Christ and His Church in the desperate medical needs of a suffering world? Peter and Hope had already shared this vision with the Council earlier, and the MMA had started giving grants to missionary midwives and nurses during post graduate courses whilst on leave from the missionfield.

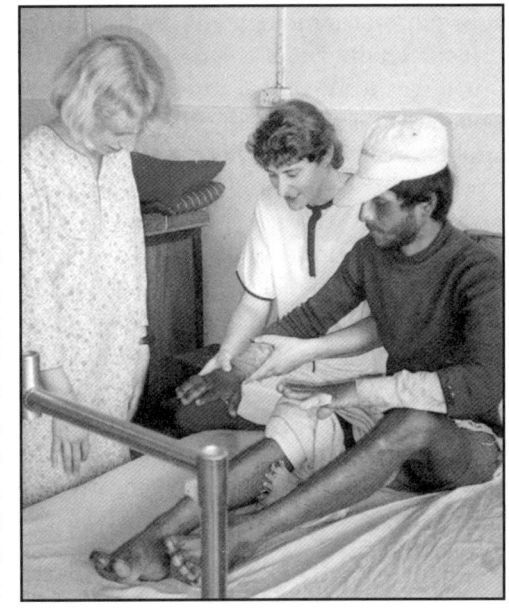

Two Therapists examining a patient in a Nepal hospital.

So it was that in April 1995, Dr David Clegg, the newly appointed Secretary, met with Mr Peter Chapman, a Christian Management Consultant and Chartered Accountant. He had been so helpful to other missionary societies, advising them on their business plans and management structures. He seemed to be just the right person to help us at this time. So, after further discussion and specific prayer, the Council decided to invite Mr Peter Chapman to examine our aims and activities in the light of the changing face of medical mission, then to present his report to the Council. Hence, in July 1995, the 'Chapman Report' was presented. It was to have a far reaching effect on the whole future of the MMA and eventually led to an exciting and challenging 'Development Plan'. The end result of this Report meant a whole new direction for the future work of the Association.

So, in 1996, after much prayer and discussion, a decision was finally made to actively involve as many members of the Council as possible with one or more of the different aspects of a future development programme. Council members were asked to volunteer their experiences in areas like Information technology, Publications and Fund raising.

If the challenge of the desperate need to health care in the developing world was to be met, a much larger income would be necessary for the Association. Fund raising therefore, would be one of the aspects of vital importance. Without hesitation, James was approached to consider this aspect as his responsibility. With his previous experience of fund raising, both with ECHO and with the King's Highway Trust, he seemed to be the obvious choice for this job!

As President, he felt constrained to accept such a challenge, although, at the moment, he would be unable to commit himself in a full-time capacity. He would endeavour to do all that he could in what ever time he had available between commitments to his medical practice. Medical missionary work had, and always would be, the prime motivation of our lives. Perhaps the time had now come for us to consider devoting our remaining work years, fully committed, back into the area to which God had called us so many years ago. The medical practice was now very much at stake!

It soon became apparent however, that this new fund raising task was going to need our full time attention if we were to do it justice and tap the vast resources of good will towards medical missionary work. So, after much prayerful consideration, a very clear call came to us. James now decided that the time had finally come for him to "hang up his stethoscope" and lay down the responsibilities of his medical practice. In so doing he would then be free to give all his available time to concentrate on fund raising and his presidential duties for the Medical Missionary Association. Together, we would be able to spend full time on a fund raising programme and seek to promote further interest and support in the work of the MMA. We had always worked closely together in the Lord's service since teenage years. Thus we would be able to finish our careers together, as we had begun them together, in medical missionary service.

But before any major steps could be taken, there were many ends to tie up and various formalities to settle; this all took time. Nevertheless, James was not going to waste any time. Fund raising was to be his specific, allocated task in the new MMA Development programme, and he wanted to play his part to the best of his ability. So to begin with, albeit part time, he started developing a certain amount of MMA fund raising before the formalities of laying down the medical practice had taken place. Our life style was about to change direction once more as we faced up to a new and exciting challenge for which we felt God had been preparing us over the years.

There was now nothing to prevent us from moving nearer to our family, so without further delay, we rented a house in the village of Downton, near Salisbury, just 5 miles from our daughter, Josephine and her family. Arrangements were made with the MMA for us to organise a small 'branch' office from which to operate our service with the Association. This would save us the long journey to London, where the main headquarters of the Medical Missionary Association was based.

As soon as the 'office' was set up, we immediately started into our first task, which was to be a massive fund raising programme. This would enable the MMA to increase its finances, which would be very necessary if they were to carry out the new thoughts and ideas that had been planned by the Council of the MMA, to expand their ministry. Thus the 'Millennium Appeal' was launched, and we began an exciting task that was to take the MMA into the 21st century and into a new era of service to a needy world.

….oOo….

29 : HealthServe is born

We soon got our little 'office' into action and, without delay, started to contact appropriate Trusts for financial help to 'set the ball rolling'. In order to contact the Christian health professionals around the country, MMA would need to employ a Travelling Secretary to assist Dr David Clegg, the General Secretary of the Medical Missionary Association. Opportunities to share the new development of the Association were already opening up around the country and we did not want to waste any time.

It was not long before James and I were ourselves, able to visit many gatherings of Christian health professionals arranged for us by regional secretaries of the Christian Medical Fellowship. On some of these occasions James had the privilege of speaking to a wider group of Christian health professionals; doctors, nurses, dentists, midwives, physiotherapists, radiographers etc; challenging them to face up to the call of God on their lives and professions.

One gathering in particular was very special; it was an unforgettable experience, infact. It was the annual medical student conference of the Christian Medial Fellowship, held at High Leigh Conference Centre. There were 350 students from medical schools in the UK, and overseas. During the missionary forum, James gave out a challenge to these young people and our hearts sang with praise as over 70 stood quietly during a time of prayer, to commit their lives and their professions to God, wherever He called them to go. Who knows what influence these committed young Christians will have on Christian medical services throughout the world?

Missionary Societies involved in medical work overseas, together with a variety of church groups, began to show an interest in MMA's developing medical programmes and it soon became obvious that we really did need someone who could spend time travelling up and down the country, while we concentrated on fund raising to support this need.

So it was that through the generous giving of so many MMA supporters and interested Trusts and Foundations, the Council was soon able to appoint **two** part time Travelling Secretaries, both doctors, whose responsibilities were to alert, inform and challenge all health professionals about mounting healthcare needs worldwide. In particular, they were asked to circulate among the younger members of the profession in hospitals and medical colleges. At the same time, we wanted to inform and challenge older health professionals, many of whom were contemplating retirement, but were at the height of their experience and expertise. Could any of them help out for short periods overseas, wherever the need was greatest, to relieve medical staff for furlough or study periods? We had, ourselves, spent 3 month in Liberia on such an exercise, so were in a good position to make the suggestion!

As interest continued to grow, a two day 'Medical Mission Summit' was organised with the Overseas Services Committee of the Christian Medical Fellowship. Thirty six people representing a range of missionary societies and church groups attended. This was thought to be the first gathering of its kind since the great Edinburgh Missionary Conference of 1910, which had led to a great surge of missionary activity at that time. Our prayer was that this 1998 'Summit' would have a similar effect, with a new army of medical missionaries taking the Gospel message and the compassion of Christ to a world of vast medical needs.

Working groups at the summit made a number of proposals and a follow up 'steering' group was set up. The overall outcome of the summit led to the idea of a 'Christian Health Professional Resource Centre' which could be developed to promote medical mission, and serve those called by God to dedicate part or all of their lives to this work. We were so privileged to have Mr Howard Lyons, the new Chairman of the MMA Council, with his extensive qualifications and experience of healthcare management. He was able to guide the Council in their planning and give advice to the steering group. This important summit was indeed a great success and a wonderful encouragement to us all.

Following the summit, a remarkable sense of collaboration and partnership developed between MMA and CMF, as together they sought to discern the best way of mobilising healthcare professionals to serve Christ and His Church in developing countries. So the steering group set out to develop and expand ideas that had been debated at the summit. Thus they would be able to create a Resource Centre that would provide a service to all churches, organisations and individuals, who had an interest in medical mission. It was evident that whilst there appeared to be wide spread support for such a centre, a lot of work still needed to be done if this was to become a reality. Finance alone, needed to be taken into consideration; there would be need for further office equipment for a start!

Now that we had managed in our fund raising programme to enable the Council to establish two Travelling Secretaries, we now had to step up our efforts and appeal for help in the region of office equipment from the appropriate Trusts that were geared to assist in this particular area. This called for a great deal of research through many fund raising directories. Quite a number of Trusts that we approached were sympathetic and many responded in a practical way, enabling the Council to go ahead with yet a further step of development towards the Resource Centre project.

While all this was going on, so was another development. This was the extension of MMA's help to medical students with their 'elective' experience, which was now part of their university degree training. This was normally carried out in a medical situation at a recognised missionary hospital overseas. In certain cases MMA would give a grant to help these students and many found this experience invaluable. In most cases it proved to be life changing, often meaning that after qualification and post graduate experience, they would return overseas at the call of God.

With the new vision of MMA to expand its ministry, further research had to be made. All branches of the medical profession would now be included and not just doctors as in the past days of the Association. There were now Christian nurses and therapy students training for university degrees who also had the opportunities of 'elective' periods. Could they not have assistance from the MMA too?

Ruth Smith - 'elective' at Tumutumu Hospital, Kenya,

It was a great joy to us personally, when the very first elective grant to a Christian undergraduate nurse was made to our own granddaughter, Ruth. She was able to go for her elective period to the Church of Scotland Hospital at Tumutumu in Kenya, to work in her degree speciality of paediatrics. Finding muddy water, or no water at all in the Childrens' ward taps, opened her eyes wide! This so concerned her, that on return to the UK, she helped the fellowship in her home church, to raise £3500 to install proper running water and storage tanks for the hospital. Truly a missionary at heart! Then following a graduate grant from the MMA, she was able to take a diploma in Tropical Nursing at the London School of Tropical Medicine. She subsequently returned again to Tumutumu to see the new water system in action before returning to gain further post graduate experience at the Birmingham Childrens' Hospital. She was the first of many more nursing and therapy students to have the life changing experience of working in a mission hospital during their elective training.

The Council now had a great deal to think about as they planned the way ahead to create a Resource Centre. After much prayer, they decided to name this new project, 'HealthServe'. It would therefore be created under the auspices and charitable status of the Medical Missionary Association. Finally, they decided to call a further 'summit' to discuss with the earlier participants of the first summit, the whole enterprise.

So on 18th February 1999, over 60 representatives from about 50 organisations involved in healthcare overseas, met together to plan the future of this new enterprise. Following reports and discussions, 'HealthServe' was enthusiastically adopted and the 'go ahead' given for the final planning and launch. The MMA accepted the responsibility of setting up and staffing the project for its first two years, after which time it was anticipated that it could become self supported by the many organisations using its services.

Following this second summit, HealthServe never looked back. This enterprise was to be a major catalyst, and have a dynamic role in Christian healthcare worldwide. It really was a tremendous undertaking in faith and its needs financially, would easily surpass our original fund raising target of £100,000. There was a tremendous lot to be done and organise. To start with, an accurate set of aims had to be decided, so that folk knew exactly what 'HealthServe' actually stood for. It would have to provide a high quality information service for Churches, Christian organisations and healthcare workers in all branches of the medical profession. This would also include students and retired professionals. There would need to be an up to date database of Christian healthcare workers in the UK (of which there are nearly 100,000!) Another aspect of the Centre would be to establish and maintain a channel of communication with overseas churches and organisations involved in healthcare mission, to assess their needs for help. With these two issues in place, it would then be possible to match the needs, with those Christian health professionals willing and free to help where the need was greatest. With a vision and task as great as this, the years 1999 and 2000 meant that there were great changes and advances in the work of the Medical Missionary Association.

Alex Wilkins 'elective' at Kapsowar Hospital, Kenya. (now graduated)

We realised that such a major undertaking as HealthServe would demand a very major increase in the annual income of the MMA, at least for the next two years. So it was, with the approval of the Council, James started an MMA Millennium Appeal Fund, for any who wished to support the establishment of HealthServe in any way. As we watched, with bated breath, the total of the Appeal crept up and up. Soon it was passing the original target of £100,000 and we had specific cause to give glory and thanks to God as we realised yet again, that 'all things are possible' with Him. If our faith is strong enough, we should accept the fact that God's work will never be short of funds; it only needs faith and trust and belief in a generous God. Now, we would put every effort, together with our faith and trust, to raise the next £100,000 necessary to get HealthServe well and truly off the ground.

At this point, the Council felt it was necessary to start considering the coming need for a Director to take over the supervision and development of HealthServe; so the search was on to find the man or woman of God's choice, to lead the new venture of HealthServe. This took time, and many fine applicants were considered. Finally, in January 2000, Mr Steven Fouch was appointed and agreed to tackle the marathon task of setting up this whole new enterprise. Steve, as he was affectionately known, was a highly qualified health professional in the nursing world. He had also worked for several years with the Christian Aids Charity ACET helping them in their effort to develop and provide services for people living with HIV and AIDS in London. He proved the ideal man for the job.

Initially Steve and his database manager Hiliary Steele, and Dr Clegg the General Secretary with his PA and office administrator, all had to share small offices in Partnership House (headquarters of the CMF) together with the CMF staff. It was impossible; this arrangement proved far too cramped! A quart will not go into a pint pot! So the next urgent issue to be sorted; 'What shall we do about office accommodation?'

Thus a hunt for alternative accommodation ensued, and after quite a short period of time, this was found in Shadwell, East London, easily accessible by the dockland light railway. These offices offered considerably more space than our small office accommodation at Partnership House, and would afford an excellent opportunity to develop and expand the whole project of HealthServe. So sadly, we had to say farewell to the Christian Medical Fellowship with whom we had had such happy co-operation and fellowship.

So in March 2000 MMA moved to Shadwell and now we were all set to launch the exciting new venture of HealthServe. Now established in their new offices, the team was all set for 'take off'! Much hard work and planning, however, was yet to be necessary before the God given vision of HealthServe was to be realised in its full potential. We were all conscious of God's presence in all of this; He was blessing the efforts of all concerned and only the future would tell the complete story of HealthServe. His purpose for the whole enterprise was surely to relieve the suffering of a desperately sick world. Ours had been the privilege in playing just a small part, as His instruments, to carry out His plan in conveying the love of Christ to our brothers and sisters in less fortunate parts of the world.

We pray that many will hear the call of God and find in HealthServe the guidance and help they need for a life given in service to the Lord Jesus Christ.

....oOo....

30 : We are all born to serve

HealthServe was now becoming established and adequate finances were enabling the whole operation to function efficiently. Hundreds of Christian health professionals from all over the UK were responding and registering on the datebase. Regular medical mission programmes and emergency health needs from the developing world were building up on the records and the whole enterprise looked set to develop into a thrilling aid programme of enthusiastic health professionals, born to serve in desperately needy situations around the world.

Now in the year 2001, we began to realise that our fund raising days were drawing to a close. We had worked our way through the Medical Missionary Association's Millennium Appeal which had originally been created to fund the Association's new plans and developments in response to the need for Christian medical care worldwide. It had started off by enabling the organisation to employ two Travelling Secretaries, and it had gone on to bring in financial help for office equipment and other general expenses needed to set up the whole enterprise. Then finally, as the vision of HealthServe evolved, designed to face up to the growing medical developments overseas, the Appeal target had been stepped up from £100,000 to £200,000, in order to meet the added expenditure of a completely independent office department and all the necessary computer, datebase and modern technology necessary for such an undertaking.

By the year 2000 it had been possible to select a Director to head up the proposed Centre together with the necessary ancillary staff. By the start of the year 2001, £160,000 had been raised, and we realised that we only had a few months left to raise the extra £40,000 before the Appeal would finally have to close. So now we were beginning to think seriously, that the time of our retirement really was about to be a reality!

As we look back over the years, it is possible to see God's pattern for our lives. As we had trained for our missionary ministry in Africa, we had been brought to a vivid realisation of the tremendous poverty and need in the poorer countries of the developing world. Then, through suffering and disappointment, God had used us to do something about this situation in the formation and development to ECHO. Here we had learnt how to fund raise in order to make ECHO into a medical supply organisation, capable of a vast and growing Centre of aid to a needy world.

Interim periods of further experience built us up to play a part in the Medical Missionary Association. Now, we were not responsible for helping to send medical equipment to needy areas overseas, but involved in an organisation that was attempting to encourage medical personnel to help, with the equipment, using their expertise in so many areas in the world, not only needing medical care, but who needed the comfort and love of Jesus. This could only be given by His disciples who were willing to realise that their role in this unhappy world, was to serve Him, their Master and Lord.

The title of this book is 'Born to Serve'. That does not just refer to anyone specific, but to ALL who claim to 'Follow Jesus'. As He chose you, so you must chose Him and in so doing, you must realise that you have been born into this world for a purpose. Then, as you claim to be a follower of Jesus, you must seek Him in quietness and confidence, so that He can reveal to you what your service for Him should be.

However, retirement for us would not mean 'switching off' completely. We would have a final fling before we passed on our fund raising responsibilities. The opportunity arose for us to visit South Africa and we would make the most of it! We would plan to contact various MMA supporters in that land, also friends in specific churches. We would make a final effort to promote and launch the HealthServe project and so enthuse any health professionals we might contact.

This then, is the end of our story as you come to the end of this book. We will not vegetate, but will always anticipate being available to our Lord and Master if He has other further specific jobs He wants us to undertake. We will always be ready to challenge those who will listen to the desperate call from the churches overseas. We will always consider Africa in the heart of all our thinking, because this really, is where it all began.

Throughout our story you will have experienced with us, the ups and downs through which we have passed; but I trust that you will also have experienced the joy and privilege which has been ours as we have seen the extent to which God's work has developed in the areas to which He has called us; two very ordinary people. We have always endeavoured to be in a position where we have been prepared to completely trust the One who has called us to 'leave our nets and follow Him'!. We have always tried to be prepared to go wherever He would lead us, through the power and strength of His Holy Spirit. It has not always been easy to know how things would work out, especially when the way appeared unusual and strange. It has often been difficult to understand what God has had in mind, and what His plans and purposes were to be.

Surely it was our God however, who drew us together to serve in partnership way back in the war years, then on to the dense jungle regions of Africa, teaching and preparing us for the responsibilities with which He had planned to entrust us in the days ahead, through testing and trial, sickness and health.

Surely God knows and understands situations before we can even begin to think or consider them ahead of time. He knew how greatly His children in the Third World were going to suffer and need help. Surely it was our God who brought ECHO into being at such a time as this, helping people we shall never see; saving lives we will never know.

Surely it was our God who caused the iron curtain to fall, opening up Eastern Europe to the Gospel and the message of God's love and the saving power of our Lord and Saviour Jesus Christ. Surely He put that burning desire into the hearts of the people for the Word of God. Surely He inspired the King's Highway Trust and Love Russia into being, giving inspiration to help those people in their needs.

Surely it was God who inspired those early doctors in 1878 to create and establish the valuable work of the Medical Missionary Association, helping to train and assist young doctors to 'go to the uttermost parts of the earth' with their medical skills and expertise. Surely it was our God who enabled us to receive the necessary experience to help in the establishment of HealthServe, which was going to be invaluable in the desperate growing medical needs worldwide. What a privilege and experience it has all been.

God has indeed been in control throughout all our experiences together in His service; we would not have had it any other way. He has given abundant strength, wisdom and determination, and we can only give Him all glory, honour and praise.

As you have read through the pages of this book, our greatest desire is that you will have seen, through all the experiences, that God can use anyone He chooses to slot into one of His programmes. The only price to pay is that you are not only willing to be slotted in, but that you do something about your willingness, and don't just stand still.

Our prayer is that you have been challenged, enthused and encouraged to serve a great God. You will have no regrets if you follow each step of the way he leads, in confidence, trust and love. You will have problems and disappointments but you will have moments of exhilaration too, and there will be resting places along the way. Surely our God will never forsake you, and will never expect you to go through more trials, problems or suffering than you can bear. He knows your weaknesses and He knows your potentials. What more could you wish for than to follow a God who turns impossibilities into possibilities, giving you the ability to do things you would never normally consider? Remember, you were born for a purpose which you may not recognise immediately. Cherish every experience and value every gift God has given you. Then go forth to serve your Lord and Master, Jesus Christ. Give Him all honour and glory, and experience the joy that this can bring. Remember, you are BORN TO SERVE and there is no better purpose in life than to follow in the way He leads.

'Oh, what a wonderful God we have! How great are His wisdom and knowledge and riches! How impossible it is for us to understand His decisions and His methods! For who among us can know the mind of the Lord? Who knows enough to be His counsellor and guide? And who could ever offer to the Lord enough to induce Him to act? For everything comes from God alone. Everything lives by His power, and everything is for His glory. To him be glory ever more.

Romans 12 v33-36

(Living Bible)

....oOo....

Glossary

Belgian Congo	-	now Democratic Republic of Congo
Leopoldville	-	now Kinshasa
Coquilhatville	-	now Mbandaka
Stanleyville	-	now Kisangani
CBMS	-	Conference of British Missionary Societies
BMS	-	Baptist Missionary Society
JMHEB	-	Joint Mission Hospital Equipment Board
ECHO	-	Equipment for Charity Hospitals Overseas
HIV	-	Human Immune Deficiency Virus
AIDS	-	Acquired Immune Deficiency Syndrone
ELWA	-	Eternal Love Winning Africa
MMA	-	Medical Missionary Association
EMMS	-	Edinburgh Medical Missionary Society
OYSTERS	-	One Year's Service to Encourage Recruiting
CMF	-	Christian Medical Fellowship

Other books by the same author

Mwanza
Flying Forceps
Cheaper by the Million
Lifeline to Millions
Children's books and stories
Children's Bible story painting books
Challenged to Conquer (autobiography)

KING'S HIGHWAY SERIES
Commandments for Travellers
Promises for Travellers
Search the Scriptures
Led by the Shepherd
Follow the Shepherd